T0367756

The Impact of International Debt Relief

International debt relief continues to be a highly controversial subject. Although many heavily indebted poor countries (HIPCs) have received large amounts of debt relief over the past quarter of a century, it does not appear to be enough. This book examines the impact of international debt relief efforts since 1990 and assesses whether the various debt relief modalities have enhanced economic growth in eight highly indebted countries in Latin America and Africa. It looks not only at the impact of possibly freed resources by debt relief but also examines the effect of a reduction of the debt stock on new capital inflows and investment and of the conditions attached to debt relief.

In comparison with other studies on debt and debt relief, the author of this book adopts a longer term perspective and analyses debt issues in a comprehensive way, including both the creditor and the debtor side. She concludes that the impact of debt relief in the 1990s was limited for various reasons, including insufficient amounts, inappropriate modalities and several unintended or even negative effects of the conditions attached to debt relief such as adverse selection and inappropriateness of conditions. Since 1999, the enhanced initiative for HIPCs and other more recent initiatives have provided more extensive debt relief in more appropriate modalities. However, a relatively small group of countries has benefited fully, and the other issues remain unresolved. Dijkstra argues that fundamental changes of the international aid and debt architecture are necessary to stop the flow of new multilateral loans and the possible perverse effects of conditionality.

Covering subject areas such as debt relief and sustainability, international financial institutions and international aid and debt architecture, this book is required reading for courses on the economics of development, global governance and development issues in general. It will also be useful to staff in international aid agencies and financial institutions.

A. Geske Dijkstra is Associate Professor in Economics at the Programme of Public Administration, Erasmus University Rotterdam.

Routledge studies in development economics

The Impact of International Debt Relief

A. Geske Dijkstra

Routledge
Taylor & Francis Group

LONDON AND NEW YORK

First published 2008
by Routledge
2 Park Square, Milton Park, Abingdon, Oxon OX14 4RN

Simultaneously published in the USA and Canada
by Routledge
605 Third Avenue, New York, NY 10017

Routledge is an imprint of the Taylor & Francis Group, an informa business

© 2008 A. Geske Dijkstra

Typeset in Times by Wearset Ltd, Boldon, Tyne and Wear
Printed and bound in Great Britain by TJI Digital, Padstow, Cornwall

British Library Cataloguing in Publication Data
A catalogue record for this book is available from the British
Library

Library of Congress Cataloging in Publication Data
A catalog record for this book has been requested

ISBN13: 978-0-415-41457-9 (hbk)
ISBN13: 978-0-203-93623-8 (ebk)

To Tom, Susanne and Wieteke

Contents

Illustrations

Figures

Tables

About the author

Anneke Geske Dijkstra studied Economics and Sociology at the University of Groningen, where she also obtained her Phd in Economics in 1988. After working several years in research institutes in Central America, back in the Netherlands, she has worked with the University of Maastricht and the Institute of Social Studies in The Hague, among other institutions. She joined Erasmus University in 2000 and is currently Associate Professor in Economics at the Programme of Public Administration. She combines research and teaching with carrying out studies and consultancies for organizations involved in development co-operation, such as the World Bank, the Swedish International Development Agency and the Dutch Ministry of Foreign Affairs. Her research interests evolve around issues of economic development, focusing in particular on aid effectiveness, economic liberalization, debt issues and gender equality. She published, among other books and articles, *Gender and economics: A European perspective*, edited with Janneke Plantenga (Routledge, 1997), *Towards sustainable development in Central America and the Caribbean*, edited with Anders Danielson (Palgrave Macmillan, 2001), *Programme aid and development: Beyond conditionality*, with Howard White (Routledge, 2003) and *Governance and the democratic deficit*, edited with Victor Bekkers, Arthur Edwards and Menno Fenger (Ashgate, 2007).

Preface

This book has its origin in an evaluation of the effectiveness of international debt relief carried out for the Operations Evaluation Department (IOB) of the Dutch Ministry of Foreign Affairs, for which the author was the lead consultant. The evaluation comprised eight country studies, an econometric study and a separate study of Dutch debt relief policies. The synthesis report on which the core of this book is based contained the results of the country studies and of the econometric study and has been written by the present author. In addition, this book contains a substantial amount of new information and analysis.

The author wishes to thank the IOB for initiating this study of debt relief and for trusting her in carrying it out. The author is particularly grateful to Dick van der Hoek who was responsible for this study at IOB and who in fact had a substantial influence on this book by his important contribution to the evaluation methodology, by his support and patience during the whole process and by his thoughtful, valuable and stimulating comments to each and every chapter of the synthesis report.

Thanks are also due to all persons who (co-)authored the country studies and the econometric study of the evaluation, in particular Eisa Abdelgalil who was then with the Foundation for Economic Research Rotterdam (SEOR), Willem Cornelissen of SEOR, Anders Danielson, then with the Faculty of Economics of the University of Lund, Trevor Evans of the Faculty of Economics of the FHTW in Berlin, Niels Hermes of the Faculty of Management and Organization of the University of Groningen and Marianne Lindner who was then with ETC Crystal. They have provided valuable information and numerous insights without which the synthesis report and the book could not have been written.

The further elaboration of the ideas and conclusions from the evaluation and their updating and application to recent debt relief initiatives has benefited from the possibility to present and discuss these ideas in several conferences and seminars. The author is grateful for many stimulating discussions with and critical comments from academics, policy makers and NGO representatives. Of course the usual disclaimer applies.

A. Geske Dijkstra

Abbreviations

AfDB	African Development Bank
BWI	Bretton Woods Institutions
DRF	Debt Reduction Facility (IDA)
DSA	Debt Sustainability Analysis
DSA	Debt Sustainability Framework
ECA	Export Credit Agency
ESAF	Enhanced Structural Adjustment Facility
FDI	Foreign Direct Investment
GDF	Global Development Finance (databank, World Bank)
GDP	Gross Domestic Product
GMM	General Methods of Moments
GNP	Gross National Product
HIPC	Heavily Indebted Poor Country
IDA	International Development Association
IDB	Inter-American Development Bank
IEG	Independent Evaluation Group (World Bank, from 2005)
IEO	Independent Evaluation Office (IMF)
IFI	International Financial Institution
IFC	International Finance Corporation
IMF	International Monetary Fund
IOB	Inspectie Ontwikkelingssamenwerking en Beleidsevaluatie (Policy and Operations Evaluation Department) – Netherlands
LDOD	Long-term debt outstanding and disbursed
MDF	Multilateral Debt Fund
MDRI	Multilateral Debt Relief Initiative
NPV	Net Present Value
NGO	Non Governmental Organisation
ODA	Official Development Assistance
OED	Operations Evaluation Department (World Bank, until 2005)

OLS	Ordinary Least Squares
PPG	Public and Publicly Guaranteed Debt
PRGF	Poverty Reduction and Growth Facility
PRSC	Poverty Reduction Strategy Credit
PRSP	Poverty Reduction Strategy Paper
SAF	Structural Adjustment Facility
UNCTAD	United Nations Conference on Trade and Development
WB	World Bank
WDI	World Development Indicators (databank, World Bank)

1 Introduction

The aim of this book is to evaluate the results of international debt relief efforts since 1990 and, in particular, their effects on the recipient countries. Debt relief continues to be a highly controversial subject. Although many heavily indebted poor countries (HIPCs) have received large amounts of debt relief over the past 25 years, they still seem to need more. Apparently, the effects have not always been favourable. From this, two contradictory conclusions can be drawn. Some argue that the international community has done far too little in alleviating the debt burden of poor countries. They have been given just sufficient relief to enable them to pay their primary creditors but not enough to allow their economies to grow, let alone to reduce poverty (Sachs 2002). International non-governmental organizations (NGOs), supported by several academic authors argue that more debt relief is necessary, especially in order to achieve the UN Millennium Development Goals[1] by the year 2015 (Berlage *et al.* 2003; Hertz 2004; Sachs 2005). Others conclude that too much relief has already been given. They argue that the most heavily indebted countries are also countries with bad policies and weak institutions, so that in the past the greatest relief has gone to countries with bad policies or without good governance (Easterly 2002; Neumayer 2002; Asiedu 2003).

However, very few studies have explicitly examined the effectiveness of debt relief. There was an early boom in studies on sovereign debt and debt relief at the end of the 1980s and in the early 1990s, when most debts were owed to private creditors. These studies are only partially relevant for the current debt problems, which are principally a problem of poor countries that owe most of their debts to official creditors. The launch of the enhanced initiative for the HIPCs (HIPC initiative) in 1999 has given a new impetus to studies on debt and debt relief. These studies broadly fall apart in four groups.

First, there are econometric studies that investigate the relationship between high debts and economic growth. Although not focusing on debt relief directly, they are useful for the debt relief debate as they shed light on the potential relevance of debt relief for economic growth (Pattillo *et al.* 2002; Clements *et al.* 2003; Pattillo *et al.* 2004; Schclarek 2004; Imbs and Ranciere 2005; Presbitero 2005).[2] Second, empirical studies have examined the allocation of debt relief (Easterly 2002; Neumayer 2002; Depetris Chauvin and Kraay 2006) and the extent of additionality of debt relief in relation to regular (other) aid flows (Powell 2003; Ndikumana 2004). Third, some evaluations have appeared of the effects of the HIPC initiative (OED 2003; Cohen *et al.* 2004; IEG 2006). Fourth, there is – to my knowledge – one econometric study of the effectiveness of debt relief (Depetris Chauvin and Kraay 2005).

This book contains elements of all four approaches but has a few distinct characteristics that add to the present knowledge. First, many recent studies and evaluations of debt relief tend to heavily focus on one aspect of debt relief, namely the reduction of the debt service and the possible benefits of the released resources for, especially, poverty reduction. In the terminology used in this book, this is known as the 'flow effect'. This book also examines two other possible effects of debt relief: the effect of a reduction in the size of the debt, independently of whether debt service declines or not, and the effect of the conditions attached to debt relief. The former is called in this book the 'stock effect' of debt relief and the latter the 'conditionality effect'. A reduction in the debt stock reduces the so-called 'debt overhang'. As will be explained later in this chapter, this term indicates that the debt has become so large that the creditors no longer expect that it will be repaid in full. As debt overhang decreases, higher debt payments can be made on the remaining debt.

Second, this book applies a relatively long time perspective. It examines the origin and causes of debt problems in general and then assesses the efficiency, effectiveness and relevance of debt relief received as from 1990s and up to and including the effects of the HIPC initiative thus far. This means it has a longer time horizon than the studies and evaluations of the HIPC initiative, which means that more can be learnt from past experiences. Third, in analysing the origins and causes of debt problems, it recognizes that loan and debt contracts originate from two parties. Too high debts are not just the result of irresponsible borrowing but may also be due to irresponsible lending. This book continues to examine the creditor side in analysing the effectiveness of debt relief. While most authors tend to focus on the possible moral hazard among the receivers of debt relief, i.e. the prospect of relief will encourage short time horizons and irresponsible borrowing (Easterly 2002; Moss and Chiang 2003) and together with defensive lending and defensive granting may induce adverse selection (Birdsall *et al.* 2003; Marchesi and Missale 2004), this book also examines possible moral hazard and causes of adverse selection on the part of the suppliers of debt relief or in the system of conditionality that has been set up for international debt relief efforts.

Fourth, this book follows eight debtor countries in particular. The detailed case study approach allows examining different effects of different modalities of debt relief as well as different effects of debt relief under different circumstances. The effects of debt relief vary according to the type of debt (concessional and non-concessional) and the type of creditor (private, official multilateral and official bilateral), according to whether debt relief concerns rescheduling (postponement) of obligations or forgiveness and to whether the relief is given on debt stocks or on debt service. The effect also varies according to the circumstances of the recipient. For example, a reduction of principal or of debt service that so far has not been paid does not increase the amount of resources in the debtor country. On the contrary, a precondition for an agreement on debt reduction is usually that the remaining debt will be serviced in the future; in the years following such a 'relief operation', therefore, actual debt service paid may be higher than before.

These different effects are impossible to capture in an econometric analysis. Depetris Chauvin and Kraay (2005), for example, lump together all forms of debt relief by looking at the reduction in the net present value (NPV) of the debt.[3] However, the effects of debt relief may vary not only by their effect on the NPV of the debt, with rescheduling generally leading to a lower effect on the NPV than forgiveness and relief on concessional debts leading to a lower effect on the NPV than relief on commercial debts, but also by whether a debt would be paid in the absence of debt relief. This means that relief on multilateral debts, though only causing a small reduction in the NPV of debt due to their concessionality, implies a large reduction in actual debt service paid. Moreover, a rescheduling of a debt service flow, even if it does not reduce the NPV at all, may have a positive flow effect if debt service would have been paid in the absence of rescheduling. In sum, the reduction in the NPV of debt is mainly important for the stock effect of debt relief in the sense that a reduction in the NPV reduces expected payments in the future but says nothing on the possible flow effect of debt relief. Most of the outcome variables examined in their study, however, deal with flow effects: government expenditure, expenditure for health and education, etc. Not surprisingly, they conclude on limited effectiveness of debt relief.

The eight countries examined in this book are Bolivia, Jamaica, Nicaragua and Peru in Latin America and Mozambique, Tanzania, Uganda and Zambia in Africa. These eight countries have received large amounts of debt relief during the 1990s, and together they represent a wide variety of debt relief modalities and circumstances. Two of them are middle-income countries (Jamaica and Peru), while the other six proved to find themselves eligible as HIPCs at the end of the 1990s. Four of these, Bolivia, Mozambique, Tanzania and Uganda, were among the first to complete the requirements of the HIPC initiative and achieved completion point in 2001, and the other two (Nicaragua and Zambia) reached the completion point in 2004 and 2005, respectively. The eight case studies are, of course, not representative of all the debtor countries in a statistical sense, but they do reflect a fairly broad variety of debt situations and external conditions.

Methodology and data sources

The methodology for assessing the impact of debt relief is deduced from a theory-based evaluation framework. The aim is to examine whether debt relief has been (1) efficient, (2) effective and (3) relevant. In order to systematically analyse the relations between inputs, outputs, outcomes and impact, a so-called logical framework has been elaborated. Figure 1.1 shows the most important aspects of this framework and of the underlying intervention theory.

The main impact variable is economic growth (Figure 1.1). Given that many recent studies consider poverty reduction the most important goal of debt relief, this choice for economic growth as the central impact variable must be explained. Basically, there are three reasons for this. First, the relation between debt relief and the ultimate poverty reduction is very difficult to ascertain. This is already true for the flow effect of debt relief but holds even more for its stock effect. A second and more formal reason is

	Stock effect	Flow effect	Conditionality effect
Input	Various debt relief modalities		Policy conditions
Output	Debt reduction	Lower debt service	Policy reform
Outcome	• Inflow of private capital • Increased private investment	• Increased imports • Public deficit reduction or increased public spending • Increased public investment and/or increased social spending • Improved social indicators	• Inflow of private capital, increased private investment • Increased public investment and/or social spending • Improved social indicators
Impact	------------------------------- Economic growth -------------------------------		

Figure 1.1 Logical framework and intervention theory.

that poverty reduction has only become the objective for debt relief with the introduction of the enhanced HIPC initiative in 1999. Since this study begins examining the effects of debt relief as from 1990, it is not very logical to assess these efforts against a policy objective that did not exist yet. Third, it is now generally accepted that economic growth is a necessary, though not sufficient, condition for lasting (sustainable) poverty reduction. If debt relief proves to have a positive effect on economic growth, it may be assumed that it has also furthered the objective of sustainable poverty reduction. Despite its main focus on economic growth as objective variable, this book does explore possible effects on the non-income dimensions of poverty such as higher literacy rates and reduced infant mortality.

The inputs of debt relief comprise the different financial modalities of debt relief, so debt forgiveness, debt restructuring, relief on debt service flows and on outstanding debt stocks and relief on debts from different creditors: bilateral, multilateral and commercial. Many combinations of these three classifications are possible. Debt relief is usually granted if certain policy conditions are fulfilled, so the conditions also form part of the inputs.

The intervention theory of the possible effects of debt relief is the following. If debt relief is to promote economic growth, this can in principle occur in three ways. First, debt relief can lead to a reduction of the debt *stock* (output) and thus of the debt overhang, which stimulates private investment and enables the country to regain access to international private capital (outcomes), which in turn may lead to economic growth (impact). This is the stock effect. Second, debt relief can result in a fall in the debt *service* (output); funds released in this way may lead to additional imports and public expenditure in physical and social infrastructure (outcomes), which also may further economic growth: the flow effect. Third, conditions attached to debt relief may induce policy improvements (output); if the correct conditions have been set, this can lead, for example, via higher public investment and social expenditure (outcomes) to increased economic growth and poverty reduction (impact). This is the conditionality effect of debt relief.

This theory is developed on the basis of what is known in the academic literature on the reverse relationship, namely on the two ways in which a large and unsustainable debt may affect economic growth: a debt overhang effect and a liquidity effect.[4] The third effect examined is in keeping with earlier insights in the effectiveness of policy-based loans and grants (programme aid) (White 1996; White and Dijkstra 2003).

In order to analyse efficiency, inputs are compared with outputs. The outputs include the direct effects of the different financial debt relief modalities: a reduction of the debt service (a decrease in the flow of outgoing payments) and of the debt stock (a decrease in the size of the outstanding debt). A third output considered here is the implementation of policy conditions that are attached to debt relief.

The investigation into the effectiveness of debt relief is concerned with a comparison of outputs and outcomes. The latter include, first, an increased sustainability of a debt burden that had become unsustainable. In addition, the effect of a possible decrease of the debt *stock* on a reduction of the debt overhang and consequently on the increase of private investments, improved creditworthiness and increased imports of private capital is examined. This is the stock effect of debt relief. The third outcome is the flow effect. If a reduction occurs in the flow of debt payments (output) as a result of debt relief, this may have effects on the government budget in the form of lower deficits or higher expenditure and on the balance of payments in the form of higher imports. Such variables actually occupy a place between outputs and outcomes and are thus called 'intermediary flow effects'. The analysis then proceeds to look for any evidence of an increase in public investment and social expenditure. This can indicate both a positive flow effect of debt relief and a positive effect of policy conditions. Finally, the effect of a possible increase in social expenditure on the improvement of social indicators is analysed and also the effect of a possible increase in public investment on private investment (crowding in).

Research into the relevance of debt relief includes above all a comparison of realized outcomes with its principal objective, economic growth. However, it is extremely difficult to establish the exact relationship between outcomes and impact (economic growth) because so many other factors may influence economic growth; conclusions are thus drawn principally on the basis of the above-mentioned theory. If the outcomes have occurred and the relationship between them and outputs of debt relief is established, it follows from the theory that a positive influence on economic growth is likely. If the outcomes have not occurred or if no relationship with debt relief is found, it is not conceivable that debt relief has contributed to economic growth.

In the empirical analysis of efficiency and effectiveness in the country studies, relevant quantitative data are presented, and trends are analysed by presenting graphs or by applying simple quantitative analysis.

Where possible, the influence of other possible factors is taken into account. With this method – common in evaluation studies – it is not possible to establish a hard counterfactual (What would have happened without debt relief?). In other words, if the intended outputs and outcomes are observed, one cannot conclude with absolute certainty that they are the result of debt relief, let alone by how much. Conversely, if the outputs and outcomes are not observed, one cannot conclude that debt relief did not have any effect. In practice, this disadvantage can be overcome. By thoroughly analysing other possibly intervening factors and by using other academic studies on the topic and country, one can almost always draw conclusions on the causal relationship between debt relief and outputs and outcomes.

In the analysis of the eight countries, no econometrics or modelling is applied. An econometric analysis per country does not make sense given that only annual data are available and that the evaluation period is too short. Although it is possible, in principle, to apply modelling and thus simulate a counterfactual, there are several reasons why this choice has not been made. Modelling requires reliable data and stable relationships, both of which are scarce in developing countries. Constructing a model implies making assumptions on possible relationships. Given the many shocks (policy and other) that these economies experience – and which would affect the coefficients of these relationships – it would be necessary to include many structural breaks. Outcomes of a model would appear to be more scientific, while they probably just reflect the assumptions made. All in all, the benefits of modelling would probably not outweigh the efforts involved.

The case study method also has an important advantage. The approach taken in the country studies allows to examine in detail the efficiency, effectiveness and relevance of different modalities of debt relief (restructuring versus forgiveness, relief on flows versus relief on stocks) and of debt relief on different types of debt (private, multilateral and bilateral). In addition, the extent of implementation of the policy conditions can be examined.

The main data source for the quantitative data is the World Bank's Global Development Finance (GDF) databank. But other data sources have also been examined, for example, IMF statistics and local data. The latter holds, in particular, for the three countries in which field work has been conducted: Mozambique, Nicaragua and Tanzania. The effects of policy conditions are discussed most extensively for these three countries. The study further makes extensive use of the existing literature on international debt problems and debt relief.

Debt overhang

As has been mentioned earlier, debt overhang occurs when creditors anticipate that the debt will not be repaid in full (Krugman 1988). This means that expected debt payments will be lower than the value of the debt, i.e. the anticipated value is lower than the nominal present value. While

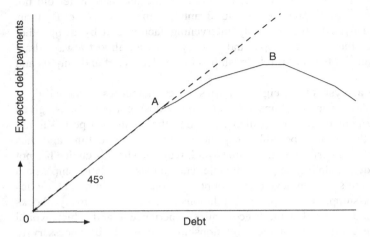

Figure 1.2 Debt overhang: the debt Laffer curve.

initially the expected value of payments equals the nominal value of the debt (between O and A in Figure 1.2), if the debt further increases, the expected payments will be less than the nominal value (between A and B). If the debt grows even further, the expected value of repayments may even *decline*. The country then finds itself in the downward section of the debt Laffer curve[5] (to the right of B in Figure 1.2). In such a situation, debt forgiveness is in the interests of both debtor and creditor. After forgiveness, the debtor will be better able to pay remaining debt service on debts that are still outstanding, and thus the actual value of remaining debt will increase.

A situation of debt overhang has several negative consequences for the debtor country (Sachs 1989). In the first place, creditors will be less willing to provide further loans, even though profitable new projects may be available. Second, the debtor country will have no incentive to invest because any proceeds from new investments will go to the old creditors. When the concept of debt overhang was first formulated, it was stressed that private investors would be discouraged: they expect taxation on investments to increase because the country, i.e. government, needs to repay its debts. But the debt overhang concept can also be interpreted more broadly (Corden 1989; Deshpande 1997). Anticipated higher debt payments not only cause higher taxes but can also lead to higher budget deficits, inflationary financing, exchange rate instability and, as a consequence thereof, capital flight. Private investment is thus discouraged by the uncertainty regarding the general macro-economic environment that accompanies a debt overhang situation. Moreover, government itself will find that proceeds from investments or from "good policies" accrue to its creditors. Debt overhang can thus also discourage good policies on the part of government.

It follows from the above that a high debt stock [e.g. in relation to gross national product (GNP)] *may* indicate the existence of debt overhang, although this is not necessarily so. How can it be ascertained in practice whether there is a case of debt overhang, i.e. a debt that creditors do not expect to be repaid in full? During the 1980s, extensive trading in debt titles took place on the secondary market which had come into existence. Their expected value could then be derived from the price of debts on the secondary market (Claessens 1990).[6] A secondary market for debts to official creditors does not exist, however, while that for private debts practically disappeared during the 1990s. It is thus difficult to deduce the actual value of official claims. Cohen (2000) made an attempt to assess the market value of the official debt at the start of the HIPC initiative. His estimate is based on the risk of non-repayment, deduced from arrears, rescheduling and refinancing of debts. He estimates that the market value is only 10 per cent, on average, of the face value, which leads him to a plea to make a distinction between nominal and actual debt cancellation in which only the latter is counted as Official Development Assistance (ODA).

A simple indicator of debt overhang that can be used for official debt is the relationship between arrears and total debt stock. When arrears are high and the country appears not to repay all debts, it is safe to assume that the expected value of the debt will increase (i.e. the debt overhang decreases) as those arrears decline. This is one of the indicators for debt overhang that will be examined in this book.

It is also possible to look at actual debt payments (i.e. flows) and, in particular, the relationship between *actual* debt repayments and payments *due*. Payments due can be calculated by summing actual debt service (DS), restructuring and forgiveness of debt service ($R + F$) and the accumulated stock of arrears (SA) (O'Connell and Soludo 2001). The ratio debt service paid/debt service due can be computed as follows:

$$\frac{DS}{DS + (R + F) + SA}$$

If this ratio of actual versus due payments is considerably less than 100 per cent, the country probably finds itself in the downward section of the debt Laffer curve (to the right of B in Figure 1.2), so there is a large debt overhang. An increase in the ratio between actual debt service and debt service due could indicate a diminishing debt overhang, so increasing creditworthiness. If debt relief causes that ratio to approximate 100 per cent, the debt overhang will be neutralized; it may then be expected that investment and good policy will no longer be discouraged and that the country will again become creditworthy. A significant obstacle to a new inflow of private capital is then removed.

The relationship between debt relief and this indicator of debt overhang is somewhat ambiguous, however. Debt relief that decreases the *stock* of outstanding debt will reduce the debt overhang (because actual payments on the smaller debt will probably increase), but debt relief that reduces the debt service (the *flow*) through forgiveness or restructuring, if it would have been paid in the absence of the relief, may increase debt overhang – it reduces the numerator, while the denominator remains constant so the ratio is reduced.[7] The debt relief modality that explicitly and most effectively reduces debt overhang in this operational definition is that of forgiveness of arrears.

A sustainable debt

An important aspect of this book is to discover whether debt relief has made the debt and the debt burden more sustainable, i.e. whether it has reduced that burden. In general, an unsustainable debt is defined as one on which future payments of interest and amortization will be so high as to affect economic growth. In the past, attempts have been made to establish empirically the magnitude of debt that is likely to cause repayment problems. For example, Cohen (1997) has determined that the ratios between debt and GNP, between debt and exports and between debt and tax revenue are good indicators of payment problems. Cohen subsequently examined the level at which these indicators would have the greatest negative impact on economic growth.

In practice, however, critical values for debt sustainability are usually measured by rule of thumb. In this book, actual values are compared with criteria applicable under the HIPC initiative. In 1999, these were made more stringent as compared to those of the original initiative (HIPC 1). The HIPC criteria, in fact, are not dissimilar to those used by Cohen (Table 1.1). One difference is that Cohen's analysis is based on nominal value and HIPC on the 'NPV'. For most low-income countries, debt ratios expressed in NPV will be lower than nominal values because a large share of their debts will be concessional. In this book, actual values are compared principally with criteria used in the enhanced HIPC initiative (HIPC 2). With regard to the debt/GNP ratio, actual values are mostly compared with the criterion applied within the European Union, namely 60 per cent. This should in fact be much lower for debts of low- and middle-income

Table 1.1 Critical values for debt sustainability ratios, in per cent

	Cohen	HIPC 1	HIPC 2
Debt/GNP	50		
Debt/export	200	200–250	150
Debt/tax revenue	300	280	250

countries, due to the much higher risk premium on interest rates that these countries are required to pay when their debt/GNP ratio is around 60 per cent (Houben 2002).

Recently, proposals have been made for stricter sustainability criteria, namely a sufficiently low debt service to allow debtor countries to attain human development (Hanlon 2000; Sachs 2002; Berlage *et al.* 2003). These authors calculate, in particular, how much in terms of resources is needed to achieve the millennium development goals. As these calculations require far-reaching assumptions (for example, on the amount of necessary spending, fiscal revenues available and other aid to be received), this book confines itself to the commonly used current debt ratios, i.e. those between debt service and exports and between debt stock and GNP.

Absolute criteria for sustainability are not needed to answer the question of whether a debt has become *more* sustainable. The significant factor is whether the debt burden has been lightened as a consequence of debt relief. Absolute criteria, in particular at the start of the study period, do matter when it comes to establishing the relevance of debt relief. Debt relief can only be the right intervention to achieve economic growth if, at that time, the debt was indeed unsustainable (i.e. could not be repaid without affecting economic growth).

In establishing the sustainability of a debt burden, a distinction can be made between indicators that measure whether countries suffer a temporary repayment problem (i.e. a lack of liquidity) and those that measure a more permanent payment problem (a lack of solvency). The distinction is, of course, relative: countries that are not solvent usually lack liquidity, while a temporary liquidity problem may become permanent if creditors lose confidence in the country's long-term growth prospects. The most important liquidity indicator is the debt service-to-export ratio. Cline (1995) argues that, in fact, it is only necessary to examine the ratio between interest payments and exports because repayment of principal simultaneously reduces liabilities. For the debt service-to-export ratio, a limit of 25 per cent is usually maintained, and for the interest-to-export ratio, this is 15 per cent. However, countries with high payment arrears may be below these critical values for actual debt service, yet they do not just suffer from temporary liquidity. Such arrears indicate long-term problems of liquidity and probably also signify that the country is not solvent. As solvency deals with the question of whether, in the long term, the country will be able to repay the debt without compromising its growth prospects, the ratios debt/GNP and debt/exports are the most important indicators.

Structure of the book

Chapter 2 briefly considers the origins of the debt problem in general and elaborates on the international responses to it to date. The causes of the debt problems of the eight countries are then discussed, including the question of whether their debts were unsustainable at the start of the study period, so 1990. The chapter then surveys the particular forms of debt relief received by the eight countries since then: the 'inputs'.

Chapters 3–5 broadly follow the logical framework, discussing the efficiency, effectiveness and relevance of debt relief for the eight countries. These chapters apply the methodology as outlined above and present the results for the period 1990–1999. The period of the application of the HIPC initiative marks a decisive change for the six countries concerned (Bolivia, Nicaragua, Mozambique, Tanzania, Uganda and Zambia). The impact of the HIPC initiative on these countries will be presented in Chapter 6, along with a brief literature survey of the effectiveness of the HIPC initiative in general.

Chapter 5, on relevance, also presents the results of an econometric analysis of the relationship between debt and growth in developing countries. It is based on data of 102 countries for the period 1970–1998 and analyses the ways in which a high debt can influence growth, giving special attention to the effect of the volatility of debt repayments. Chapter 6 compares the impact of debt relief during the 1990s with the results of debt relief provided since 2000 and assesses the prospects for the future.

2 The origins of debt and an overview of debt relief

Origins of the debt problem

The current debt problems have their origins in the 1970s. After the 1973 oil price hike, in particular, developing countries started to borrow money on a large scale from banks in industrialized nations. The literature describes extensively how both demand and supply factors played a role in this situation. The oil-rich nations deposited their sudden wealth with western banks, causing surplus liquidity among them. The rich countries were then in recession, so that the banks had few possibilities of investing their petrodollars at home. Developing countries, on the other hand, faced considerable balance-of-payments deficits due to the higher oil prices and exerted a powerful demand for credit. Moreover, the predominant development paradigm at the time was that poor countries should invest in industry, particularly import substitution industrialization, and in infrastructure and that governments must play a leading role in that respect. Consequently, money was borrowed chiefly by states (and state enterprises).

Later, problems were caused particularly by the manner and conditions under which banks lent their money. Not only were international interest rates low at the time, but the banks also charged a risk premium that was far too low. In addition, they had high concentrations of loans in certain countries – a strategy prohibited when lending to private borrowers as it entails high risks for the bank's future. Finally, the banks charged variable interest rates – rational in a time of high inflation, but also increasing the risk of default as rates rose. In general, this collective irresponsible acting (market failure) on the part of banks can be attributed to the well-known herd behaviour shown by actors on financial markets: the costs of not going with the flow are far too high for individual banks or individual analysts within the banks who prefer to ignore the risks ('countries cannot go bankrupt'). In addition, a system of regulation and control over banks' international activities did not then exist, and the banks assumed that governments would come to their rescue if they should get into difficulties. After all, they had taken on the burden of recycling petrodollars with the explicit support of their governments by channelling these surplus funds to countries that needed them (Dooley 1994).

These distortions (market failures) occurred not only on the supply side but also on the demand side (government failure). Partly due to the very low interest charged, governments of developing countries were tempted to borrow large amounts, even for projects that would not have been profitable under a normal interest rate. In Latin America, in particular, investment levels were very high between 1975 and 1982 [an average of 24 per cent of gross domestic product (GDP) higher than before 1975 and after 1982]. Some countries, however, followed a policy that was clearly irresponsible, expressed in very large government deficits, for example.

This description of the origins of high debt levels applies especially to middle-income countries and in particular to Latin America. In Africa, debt also started to grow during the 1970s, but that growth continued in the 1980s. Rather than commercial banks, the main sources of loans to Africa were official creditors, particularly the governments of industrialized nations. Here, too, distortions on the supply side played an important role. The recession of the 1970s and the emergence of foreign aid caused loans to be provided on a large scale to poor countries. On the one hand, these included export credit guarantees whereby the government of the exporting country guaranteed a commercial loan that an exporter extended to his or her buyer and, on the other hand, aid loans that, partially or wholly, were often spent in the creditor country. In both cases, the loan was not given on account of its anticipated yield, but due to a combination of need in the recipient country and the desire to promote exports from the donor country.

Although the volume of World Bank loans in particular grew rapidly during the 1970s, the role played by multilateral institutions was then still limited. This changed during the 1980s when the debt crisis really erupted. The announcement by Mexico in 1982 that it was no longer able to pay its debt service marked the start of the actual crisis. Even before that, however, various African countries had requested that their debts be restructured.

At the start of the 1980s, the high debt burdens of many low- and middle-income countries quickly became problematic due to a number of changes in the world economy. In 1979, the oil-producing countries again raised their prices, but this time the reaction by the industrialized countries was quite different. The USA and the UK, in particular, were concerned principally about inflation and far less about the fall in aggregate demand.

They introduced tight monetary policies, causing interest rates to shoot up. This led to a world-wide recession which in turn led to reduced demand for the export products of developing countries and to lower prices for those products. Debtor countries thus had to cope simultaneously with higher oil prices, higher interest rates and lower prices for their exports. In Latin America, higher interest rates formed the most important reason for the rapid debt increase; in Africa, where official creditors usually charged a fixed interest, the main cause was the deteriorating terms of trade. On both continents, the situation was further impaired by capital flight.

International responses

The debt problem was called a crisis principally because many major western banks threatened to go bankrupt, and in a few cases actually did so. Initially, until about 1984, it was assumed that debtor countries were suffering temporary payment problems and that new loans would help them to recover. The International Monetary Fund (IMF) attempted to co-ordinate the banks in granting new loans; later, in 1985, the Baker Plan[1] also aimed at mobilizing new funds for debtor countries. Meanwhile, however, the banks had arrived at a different assessment of the situation. They no longer expected that they would get their money back, refused to provide debtor countries with new loans and started to write off the old loans. They, of course, still tried to recover as much money as possible from debtor countries, while making grateful use of the funds that official creditors (multilateral and bilateral) made available to those countries (Dooley 1994). For the average Latin-American debtor country, however, the net effect was negative: they had surpluses on their balance of payments and repaid more than they received in the form of new loans and grants. The fact that multilateral institutions provided loans on a large scale led to commercial creditors being partly bailed out with official loans. At the same time, these new official loans also allowed a greater outflow of debt repayments than would otherwise have been possible (Sachs 1989).

In view of the growing provisions of commercial banks and an emerging secondary market in private debt titles, a new Secretary of the US Treasury, Nicholas Brady, announced a plan for market-based debt reduction in 1989. This plan no longer implied new loans from private creditors. Instead, it allowed debtor countries to buy back private debts at their secondary market price. Official money, mainly from the World Bank, the IMF, the USA and Japan, was provided to help these countries financing the buybacks and to collateralize exit bonds, usually US Treasury bonds (Bowe and Dean 1997).

The response of official creditors to the payment problems of debtor countries was very different from that of the commercial banks. In general, they adhered much longer to the notion that debtor countries faced only temporary liquidity problems rather than insolvency. During the 1980s, export credit agencies (ECAs) in the rich countries continued to insure commercial loans. Concessional aid loans were also continued. The net flow of bilateral loans to Africa remained positive during the 1980s. In addition, western donors started to provide grants to African countries at a growing rate. At the same time, western creditor governments, united in the Paris Club,[2] dealt with payment problems by means of rescheduling. This meant only a postponement of payment obligations while the interest was capitalized and the net present value (NPV) of the loan remained unchanged (and its nominal value increased).

Starting in 1988, official creditors also began to acknowledge that some of the loans would probably never be repaid, and they started to cancel them partially. This applied only to debts entered into before a certain date, however (the 'cut-off date', usually three years prior to the initial agreement and later unchanged), and only to the debt service due during a specific period. The percentage that was forgiven on this limited part of the debt service was gradually increased from 33 to 50 (1991), to 67 (1994) and to 80 (1996). The remainder of the debt service due was rescheduled on market terms. One condition for such an agreement with the Paris Club was that the country in question had entered into an agreement with the IMF. The agreement with the Paris Club only covered debt service obligations falling due during the course of the IMF agreement. Hence, new debt agreements were usually necessary when a new IMF programme was concluded.

Multilateral institutions such as the IMF and the World Bank strongly expanded their lending during the 1980s. In doing so, they fulfilled the role of 'lender of last resort'; by imposing policy conditions, they also tried to persuade other creditors to make funds available again. The World Bank and the IMF co-operated ever more closely in the so-called structural adjustment programmes. Starting in 1986, the IMF opened a concessional 'window' for the poorest countries: first, the Structural Adjustment Facility (SAF) and, from 1987 onwards, the Enhanced Structural Adjustment Facility (ESAF). The two institutions were preferred creditors, meaning that debtors always had to meet the debt service to these creditors first; otherwise, they would not be considered for new loans or for debt restructuring by bilateral creditors united in the Paris Club or for (part of the) aid provided by bilateral donors. During the 1990s, this obligation proved to be an unsustainable burden for many poor debtor countries. It was not until 1996, however, and more extensively in 1999 with the enhanced heavily indebted poor countries (HIPCs) initiative that the international community came to acknowledge that debt relief was also needed on multilateral debts. In 2006, the relief on multilateral debt was further expanded with the Multilateral Debt Relief Initiative (MDRI) that was first proposed during the G8 meeting in July 2005 in Scottish Gleneagles.

Although for commercial banks and for most Latin-American countries the debt crisis was over by 1990, this was by no means the case for the majority of the poorest countries and for most countries in sub-Sahara Africa. In Latin America, the average debt/gross national product (GNP) ratio started to fall considerably after 1988, but in Africa it continued to rise until 1994. Even after that it remained at over 60 per cent. Yet more evidence that the successive rescheduling agreements with the Paris Club did not solve the debt problems of poorest countries is that many of the latter returned and needed more restructuring. Sachs (2002) shows that out of the 59 countries that entered into agreements with the Paris Club between 1975 and 1996, 39 were still in need of restructuring between 1996 and 1999 while 12 still made use of an IMF facility (i.e. suffered balance-of-payments problems). Only eight countries had been 'cured', i.e. were no longer in need of either.

Why were private creditors so much quicker than their official counterparts in realizing that it was necessary to forgive debts? One reason is that private creditors and, in particular, the commercial banks are subject to regulations that force them to revalue and (partially) to write off bad debts. Official creditors are not subject to this type of oversight. Second, the market forces these private creditors to seek alternative and more profitable investments. Such considerations do not apply to official bilateral creditors. During the 1980s and much of the 1990s, they maintained the fiction that debtor countries would eventually repay most of their debts. They did not write off and forgave only part of the debt service. ECAs continued for a long time to provide poor debtor countries with guarantees. Meanwhile, however, the poorest countries had become quite unable to pay their debt service, even after rescheduling with the Paris Club. Bilateral donors thus increased their grants to such countries, and multilateral institutions expanded their concessional lending.

This combination of debt restructuring with new loans and grants was beneficial to the various stakeholders in the wealthy countries (Daseking and Powell 1999). That is the third reason for the different approach adopted by official creditors. Since ECAs did not write off bad debts, they could continue to lend, thus helping to promote exports from rich nations. The restructuring of debt service payments reduced pressure on Ministers of Development Co-operation to provide yet more aid in support of adjustment programmes. Restructuring just meant postponement of claims, and the costs were thus not (yet) covered from aid budgets. Moreover, most ministers preferred to provide new aid rather than to contribute, directly or indirectly, to the payment of the claims of their ECAs, as would probably have been the case if greater amounts of debt had been forgiven. This approach also benefited multilateral institutions, enabling them to continue to provide loans to debtor countries that were in fact no longer creditworthy. Such loans were only possible because multilateral institutions were preferred creditors and thus assured of recovering their funds.

However, the delay in acknowledging that large-scale relief was needed had a number of consequences for the allocation of aid and for its distribution among creditors. There proved to be a clear link between the size of the debt, particularly of multilateral debt, on the one hand and the volume of aid (concessional loans and grants) on the other hand. This relationship between debt forgiveness and new grants was already demonstrated for 32 sub-Saharan African countries on the basis of data for the years 1983–1993 (Hernández and Katada 1996). A more recent study also shows that on top of that, a process of adverse selection seems to have been initiated: countries with poor policies were given more aid (Birdsall *et al.* 2003). This is one of the indications for the fact that bilateral aid ministers ultimately settled the account of multilateral creditors (see Chapter 3).

Origins of debt problems in the eight countries

In five of the eight countries studied (Bolivia, Jamaica, Peru, Tanzania and Zambia), the high debt burden originated in the 1970s (Figures 2.1 and 2.2). These countries adopted a strategy of import substitution industrialization, requiring loans for investment in industry and infrastructure. That strategy also entailed the relative neglect of the agricultural sector, causing deficits on the current account of the balance of payments. These deficits were aggravated after 1974 by high oil prices and in some cases also by falling prices for the most important export products. This was particularly the case in Zambia which was very dependent on copper, but also in Tanzania (sisal) and Jamaica (bauxite, sugar). Zambia turned to the IMF in 1976 and Jamaica in 1977; Tanzania also approached the IMF in 1979 but was unable to agree to its terms. The other five countries were still reasonably able to finance their deficits throughout the 1970s.

In Nicaragua and Uganda, debts only started to climb slightly towards the end of the 1970s. Dictators were in power in both countries (Anastasio Somoza and Idi Amin, respectively), who showed no interest in development and thus did not go along with the modern vogue of large-scale externally financed investment. In Mozambique, which became independent in 1975, *recording*[3] of external debt started only in 1981.

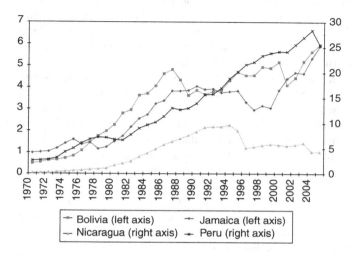

Figure 2.1 Long-term debt outstanding and disbursed (LDOD) of Bolivia,
Jamaica, Nicaragua and Peru, 1970–2005, in US$ billions (nominal)
(source: World Bank, Global Development Finance online, 2007).

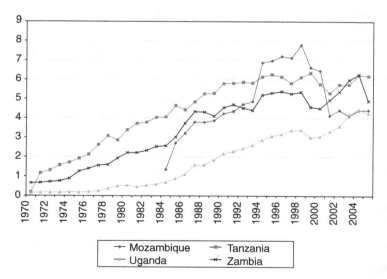

Figure 2.2 Long-term debt outstanding and disbursed (LDOD) of Mozambique,
Tanzania, Uganda and Zambia, 1970–1998, in US$ billions (nominal)
(source: World Bank, Global Development Finance online, 2007).

The growth of debts of these countries during the 1970s was made possible on the supply side by the same factors that played a role in general, namely an abundant supply of cheap loans from the western banking sector and the desire of official bilateral creditors to promote their countries' exports. But these eight countries, including those in the western hemisphere, received relatively large amounts of government loans and fewer commercial credits. In 1980, the share of commercial banks in total debt was less than half in all four Latin-American countries, which in that respect were comparable with Uganda and Zambia (see Table 2.1). In Tanzania, a 'donor darling' at the time, bilateral loans accounted for three-quarters of the total debt in 1980. Donors as it were, queued for the chance to support President Nyerere's policy of self-reliance, with the result that the country became very dependent on foreign aid.

All eight countries considered in this study saw their debts increase strongly during the 1980s. In those that were already highly indebted in 1980 and where commercial loans played a large part in that situation (Peru, Bolivia and Zambia), this was due at least in part to the sudden rise in interest rates. In all countries, the global recession and the consequent (further) deterioration of the terms of trade also played a role. In addition, a variety of factors on the demand side caused debts to increase even further.

At around 1980, Mozambique and Nicaragua introduced an import substitution industrialization policy along socialist lines which, similar to that

Table 2.1 Share of the various categories of creditors in total public debt, 1980 and 1990, in per cent

	Bilateral		Multilateral		Private		Total	
	1980	1990	1980	1990	1980	1990	1980	1990
Bolivia	30	48	20	43	49	9	100	100
Jamaica	44	57	20	30	36	13	100	100
Nicaragua	26	70	25	11	48	19	100	100
Peru	42	32	8	16	50	52	100	100
Mozambique[a]	34	74	65	11	1	15	100	100
Tanzania	75	58	17	34	8	8	100	100
Uganda	40	26	15	59	45	15	100	100
Zambia	51	59	19	31	30	10	100	100

Source: Calculated on the basis of data from World Bank: Global Development Finance, CD-ROM 2002

Note
a The 1980 column for Mozambique refers to 1981 when the size of recorded debt was still so small that little can be said about its distribution.

of Tanzania introduced a decade earlier, was largely supported with donor loans. Mozambique was then anxious to finance its development with loans rather than grants, in order to retain its independence (Bossema 1995). In 1990, the share of bilateral loans in the total debts of the two countries was almost as large as that of Tanzania in 1980 (Table 2.1). In Uganda, after the ousting of Amin, reconstruction was supported especially by multilateral institutions. The first adjustment programme started in 1984 but soon came to an end when a new civil war erupted. President Museveni, who came to power in 1986, signed an agreement with the IMF and the World Bank a year later. Although bilateral aid to Uganda also started to flow at the end of the 1980s, multilateral institutions are, by 1990, responsible for the greater part of the country's debt (59 per cent; see Table 2.1).[4]

Jamaica and Zambia underwent a series of adjustment programmes during the 1980s which were supported by bilateral and multilateral loans and thus increased the debt burden. The programmes were only partly implemented, however, and did not lead to economic recovery, due in part to the still unfavourable terms of trade. Zambia broke with the International Financial Institutions (IFIs) in 1987 over the policy to be followed; this lasted until 1991. The country was given no new loans and suspended its payments to the IFIs. As a result, the debt situation stabilized. Tanzania did not enter into an agreement with the IMF over structural adjustment until 1986. This agreement made it possible to finance balance-of-payments and fiscal deficits more easily: economic growth started to increase, but so did foreign debt.

Bolivia had already started to conclude restructuring agreements regarding debt service to private creditors in 1979, but high interest rates caused the debt to increase rapidly in the early 1980s. In 1983, the country announced that it was no longer able to pay its debts. Yet the net inflow of commercial and government funds remained positive in the first half of the 1980s, partly because bilateral creditors started to support the 'young democracy'.[5] Meanwhile, the budget deficit continued to grow, resulting in hyperinflation in 1985. A new government started to implement an orthodox adjustment policy and entered into an agreement with the IMF. Inflation then declined rapidly, but the debt continued to increase and there was little evidence of economic growth during the 1980s.

At the start of the 1980s, Peru was forced to reduce its imports since neither commercial banks nor official creditors would make further loans available. In 1985, the long-standing military regime at last came to an end, and donors began to support Alan García's new government. The latter did not sign an agreement with the IMF but followed a heterodox stabilization policy which, in practice, meant that macro-economic deficits and foreign debts increased. Arrears in debt servicing increased rapidly, and in 1987, Garcia announced a moratorium on debt payments.

As might be expected, the share of private debt in the total debt fell during the 1980s in all eight countries (Table 2.1). Peru was an exception, due particularly to arrears on private debt payments that had been mounting since 1984 and that form part of the debt stock. Banks withdrew as much as possible from the affected countries. In Bolivia, the share of private debt declined in particular as a result of a co-ordinated buyback operation of private debt carried out in 1986.

In most countries, the share of multilateral debt grew considerably in the 1980s due to successive structural adjustment programmes. In Peru, however, the increase was only slight because that country had no agreement with the IMF. In Nicaragua and Mozambique, where socialist governments were still in power, the multilateral share in total debt even decreased. The USA effectively exercised its veto power with regard to multilateral lending to these countries.

By 1990, the debt burden in all eight countries had become unsustainable when measured by conventional debt ratios (Table 2.2). Only Peru and Uganda were then slightly under the 60 per cent level that is usually considered as sustainable for the ratio between debt and national income. The other six countries were (far) above that limit, with Nicaragua at the peak with 842. In all eight countries, moreover, the debt/export ratio was higher than 150 per cent, the threshold used in the enhanced HIPC initiative. Nicaragua was again in the lead with 2,058 per cent, but for Mozambique, Tanzania and Uganda, the ratios were also very high. All this signifies that, in 1990, not one of the eight countries was solvent. With a debt/export ratio of 161 per cent, Jamaica only slightly exceeded the HIPC solvency norm of 150 per cent.

The fact that all eight countries were also experiencing liquidity problems can be seen from the high values for the debt service-to-export ratios. Only in Nicaragua, Peru and Zambia that ratio was below 25 per cent, but that was due chiefly to high arrears: arrears constituted around 50 per cent or more of the debt stock, meaning that actual payments were far less than payments due (see final row of Table 2.2). This applied also to Mozambique and Tanzania, although to a lesser degree. In 1990, Jamaica was in the most favourable situation, also in terms of liquidity.

Inputs: debt relief to the eight countries during the 1990s

Table 2.3 surveys the modalities of debt relief received by the eight countries over the years. Columns 2–8 show the years in which agreements

Table 2.2 Debt ratios in 1990 for the eight countries, in per cent

	Bolivia	Jamaica	Nicaragua	Peru	Mozambique	Tanzania	Uganda	Zambia
Debt/GNP	84	106	842	55	182	142	51	151
Debt/Export	387	161	2058	317	1411	1065	879	334
Debt service/ export	39	27	4	11	26	33	59	15
Interest payments/ export	14	11	3	6	13	11	15	6
Arrears/Debt	1	7	50	87	22	21	14	49

Source: Calculated on the basis of World Bank data, Global Development Finance, CD-ROM.

Notes

Debt: long-term debt outstanding and disbursed (LDOD); GNP: Gross National Product; Export: exports of goods and services.

Table 2.3 Summary of types of debt relief to the eight countries

(1) Countries	(2) Classic[a]	(3) Houston[b]	(4) Toronto (33%)	(5) London (50%)	(6) Naples (67%)	(7) Lyon (80%)	(8) Cologne (90%)	(9) Multilateral arrears	(10) MDF	(11) HIPC 1	(12) HIPC 2	(13) Private
Bolivia	1986		1988–1990 1992		1995–1996	1998 (stock)	2001		1996–2000	1997 Decision point 1998 Completion point	2000 Decision point 2001 Completion point	1986 Buyback 1988 Brady 1993 Buyback 1997 Buyback
Jamaica	1984, 1985 1987, 1988 1990	1991 1993										
Nicaragua				1991	1995, 1998			1991 (IDB, WB)			2000 Decision point 2004 Completion point	1995 Buyback
Peru	1968, 1969 1978, 1983 1984, 1991	1993 1996						1992 (IMF)				1996 Brady 1999 buyback 2002 buyback
Mozambique	1984	1987 (ad hoc)	1990	1993	1996	1998 1999 (stock) 2000	2001		1996–1998	1998 Decision point	2000 Decision point 2001 Completion point	1991 Buyback
Tanzania	1986		1988, 1990	1992	1997	2000	2001		1998–2000		2000 Decision point 2001 Completion point	1990–1993 Debt Swap 2001 Buyback
Uganda	1981, 1982	1987 (ad hoc)	1989	1992	1995 (stock)	1998 (stock)	2000		1996–1998	1997 Decision point 1998 Completion point	2000 Decision point 2000 Completion point	1993 Buyback

	1990	1992	1996, 1999	1991 IMF 1991 WB	2000 Decision point 2005 Completion point	1994 Buyback
Zambia						

Sources: Abdelgalil and Cornelissen 2003c; 2003a; 2003b; Danielson and Dijkstra 2003; Dijkstra 2003; Dijkstra and Evans 2003; Lindner 2003a; 2003b; GDF online 2005, and World Bank, Summary of Completed Facility Operations, December 2003, accessed 7 January 2007.

Notes

a Classic terms are limited to restructuring which leaves the real (or net present value) of the debt unchanged.
b Houston terms were introduced in 1990 for middle-income countries and comprised extension of maturities which reduced the NPV of the debt slightly.
c MDF: Multilateral Debt Fund: fed by bilateral grants and used for the payment of multilateral debt service.

were entered into with the Paris Club regarding bilateral debt. The middle-income countries Jamaica and Peru had access only to restructuring that was barely concessional, if at all (columns 2 and 3). Since 1988, an increasing percentage of debt forgiveness has been applied to eligible debt service (columns 4–7). Since the Naples terms, forgiveness of the outstanding debt itself (i.e. the stock) was allowed, while an agreement under Cologne conditions always includes a stock-of-debt treatment (columns 6–8).

Columns 9 and 10 show bilateral relief on multilateral debt service. By 1990, Nicaragua, Peru and Zambia were in arrears with multilateral institutions (column 9). These were cleared with the aid of loans and grants from bilateral creditors and donors. In addition, many countries were given bilateral grants with which to settle multilateral debt service. This often took place through a special World Bank facility, known as the fifth dimension. Bolivia, Nicaragua, Uganda, Tanzania and Zambia, in particular, benefited from this. However, it was not possible to obtain sufficient data on this during the country studies, and it is therefore not included in Table 2.3.[6] In some countries, and towards the end of the decade, such relief on multilateral debt service was co-ordinated among the donors through a Multilateral Debt Fund (MDF). This fund was usually terminated when the country qualified for the HIPC initiative (see columns 11 and 12).

Table 2.3 shows that Bolivia and Uganda have reached the completion point of HIPC 1 but subsequently also became eligible for HIPC 2. By 2006, all six HIPCs have reached the completion point of the initiative so they are entitled irrevocably to relief on debt service to the multilateral banks for the next 15 or 20 years. As from 2006, they also benefit from MDRI (not in Table 2.3) which implies 100 per cent cancellation of pre-2004 debts to the World Bank, the IMF and the African Development Bank.

The final column in Table 2.3 shows that in most countries, private debts have been bought back. In all countries, such buybacks have been financed (almost) fully with capital received through the Debt Reduction Facility (DRF) of the World Bank, also known as the sixth dimension, to which both the Bank itself and bilateral donors contribute.

Table 2.4 shows the amounts of debt relief received by the eight countries during the 1990s, based on figures in the Global Development Finance (GDF) databank (middle column).[7] It should be remembered that not all debt relief is recorded in that databank (and therefore probably, neither are all debts): in 1997, for example, Mozambique signed an agreement with the former Soviet Union regarding a considerable debt reduction, but this is not to be found in these figures.[8] In general, reductions of

Table 2.4 Debt relief received during 1990–1999, and shares of the various modalities

	Share forgiven in %	Share rescheduled in %	Total debt relief in US$ million (=100%)	Share flow relief in %	Share stock relief in %
Bolivia	49	51	2823	89	11
Jamaica	43	57	1249	92	8
Nicaragua	77	23	9338	54	46
Peru	15	85	15432	91	9
Mozambique	54	46	5111	69	31
Tanzania	53	47	2629	100	0
Uganda	74	26	1202	79	21
Zambia	41	59	3738	88	12

Source: Global Development Finance.

debts to the Soviet Union are probably underestimated in GDF data (Daseking and Powell 1999). These figures do indicate the magnitude of debt relief, however.

Peru and Nicaragua both received much debt relief, while Jamaica and Uganda had much less. By far, the greatest part of debt relief to Peru consisted of restructuring. Jamaica, which like Peru is a middle-income country, was forgiven a remarkably high proportion of its debt. In general, the share of debt forgiveness is low: only in Nicaragua and Uganda, it was clearly more than half. In all eight countries, most debt relief proved to be flow relief (rescheduling plus forgiveness on debt service due). A very small part of the total relief concerned debt stocks. Only in Nicaragua did this amount to 46 per cent.

Inputs: conditions for debt relief

During the 1980s, an agreement with the IMF on structural adjustment was a condition for new loans by commercial banks, from multilateral institutions and sometimes also from bilateral creditors. In practice, commercial banks hardly provided new loans (see also Figure 3.1 below). At the time of the market-based reduction of private debts, the contributions by official creditors to the Brady Plan were similarly tied to an IMF agreement. Such an agreement was not necessary for decisions of private banks to write off debt via reductions or discounts on the nominal value of the debt. Commercial banks were interested not so much in an IMF agreement or its implementation, as in the inflow of official capital that accompanied it and enabled the country in question to repay at least part of the claims of private creditors (Dooley 1994).

An IMF agreement was always a condition for debt relief agreements with the Paris Club on official bilateral debt. With a few exceptions and as was indicated above, such agreements were concerned with debt service only, i.e. with arrears on debt service incurred up to the date of the agreement, and with claims falling due during the term of the IMF agreement. Once the Paris Club signed an agreement, this was adhered to by its members, whether or not the debtor implemented the IMF agreement.

Bilateral contributions to an MDF were frequently linked to an IMF agreement and its successful implementation. In addition, it was important for such bilateral debt relief that the country in question should make serious efforts to control corruption, that it had an independent legal system and that it should hold free elections. In brief, these bilateral donors required good governance. Sometimes, there was also a stipulation regarding better debt management by the government (Uganda) or on the use of 'countervalue funds'.[9]

The original HIPC initiative of 1996 set only a few conditions. Countries had to be poor and highly indebted; apart from that they were required to have implemented twice a three-year adjustment programme in agreement with the IMF and the World Bank. After the first three-year period, they could reach the so-called decision point. The degree of unsustainability of the debt would then be investigated and the amount of debt relief determined. After another three years of structural adjustment, the completion point could be reached, after which the country would have complete access to all promised multilateral and bilateral debt relief.

The enhanced HIPC initiative of 1999 not only brought more debt relief for more countries but also changed the policy conditions. To reach the decision point, countries had to draw up a Poverty Reduction Strategy Paper (PRSP) in which stakeholders had to participate. After the decision point, they would have immediate access to debt relief by multilateral institutions (interim relief) which would have to be used for implementing the PRSP. The duration of the period between decision point and completion point became flexible. Instead of having completed another three-year adjustment programme successfully, the country had to at least implement a number of tangible reforms and had to start implementing a PRSP, to be certified by a progress report. On reaching the completion point, the interim relief would be continued but would now be fixed for the next 15–20 years, and bilateral creditors would forgive the greater part of their debt stocks.

In short, HIPC 1 conditionality was restricted to evaluating (ex post) the track record of past performance, while HIPC 2, in addition to (somewhat weaker) ex post conditions, set again conditions in advance (ex ante). Moreover, HIPC 2 signified that demands were set on the use of debt relief. This had not occurred previously, except for a few countries with an MDF.

All countries that have reached the completion point of HIPC 2 are eligible for the MDRI, provided there are no signs of deterioration in performance with respect to macro-economic stability or the implementation of their PRSP.

Conclusions

The causes of the debt problem may be found on both the demand and the supply side. Commercial banks did not properly estimate the risks involved and offered too low rates of interest because they had surplus liquidity. Their international activities were not subject to supervision and regulation. Creditor governments wanted to promote development in recipient countries, but also their own exports. Later, in the 1980s, the IMF and the World Bank acted more or less as lenders of last resort for debtor countries. In these cases, the decisions to lend were not taken on the basis of an appraisal of expected yields and risks. Moreover, loan applicants frequently pursued an irresponsible policy expressed, for instance, in high budget deficits and over-valued exchange rates that hampered exports.

Private creditors were far quicker than official creditors to recognize that debtor countries suffered from more than a temporary problem of liquidity and that they were actually insolvent. This was due first to the fact that, unlike governments, banks are subject to regulations that force them to write off dubious debts. ECAs continued until well into the 1980s to provide new credit guarantees to countries that could no longer meet their obligations. Second, rich countries preferred to reschedule debts and provide new aid. The recognition that the debts would never be repaid would have given rise to the difficult question out of which budget the write-off of dubious claims, including those of ECAs, would have to be financed.

In all eight countries studied, the debt problem by 1990 was already primarily one of official debt. In 1980, private debt represented between 30 and 50 per cent of the debt in six of the eight countries, but by the start of the 1990s, this share had fallen to less than 20 per cent in all but Peru. In 1990, all eight had an unsustainable debt if outstanding debt is compared with exports. Jamaica's debt was the most sustainable; in the other seven, the debt/export ratio was far above the HIPC criterion of 150 per cent.

During the 1990s, the eight countries received a broad variety of debt relief modalities. A large part of that relief, however, consisted of the rescheduling of debt service due, which did not reduce the total volume of outstanding debt. For the majority, the share of debt forgiveness in total debt relief ranged between 41 and 54 per cent. For Peru, it was much lower (15 per cent) and for Nicaragua and Uganda much higher (approximately 75 per cent). By far, the greater part of debt relief received consisted of relief on *flows* (including arrears) and far less of relief (forgiveness) on principal (*stocks*).

3 The efficiency of debt relief

This chapter attempts to answer the question of whether debt relief provided during the 1990s was efficient, i.e. whether the funds made available for the purpose were efficiently used. To this effect, 'inputs' are compared with 'outputs'. Debt relief is efficient if the funds used have reduced the debt stock and/or have led to a considerable reduction in the flow of actual debt payments. These issues will be discussed in the first two sections of this chapter.

A third 'output' consists of policy changes that donors and creditors try to bring about by setting conditions. Until 1999, the only condition attached to debt relief in the multilateral framework (Paris Club, HIPC 1) was that the country in question must have an agreement with the International Monetary Fund (IMF). This chapter therefore also discusses the implementation of the IMF agreements; first in general and then specifically for the eight countries. The final section concludes.

Reduction of the debt stock

Reduction of the debt stock can only be brought about by debt forgiveness. Restructuring leads merely to the deferment of payment; if the interest is capitalized, the nominal value of the debt will even increase.

Analyses of all debtor countries in Latin America and sub-Sahara Africa show that the various debt relief initiatives have had little effect on reducing debt stocks (Dijkstra and Hermes 2003). The implementation of market-based debt reduction on private debts led to a peak in debt forgiveness in 1988–1990 when 4–5 per cent of total debt in Latin America was cancelled each year. In Africa, where private debt formed a smaller percentage of the debt stock, a peak occurred in 1989 but of less than 3 per cent. On the other hand, Africa also reached 3 per cent during 1996–1998 when the Paris Club's forgiveness percentage had been raised to 67 per cent (later 80 per cent) of debt service; a few countries then profited from reduction of their outstanding debt stock and, in 1998 and 1999, some started to benefit from the (first) heavily indebted poor country (HIPC) initiative. In the other years, the forgiveness percentages were much lower. These general figures are averages for the region as a whole, however, i.e. they include countries that needed little debt reduction.

According to Table 2.4 above, about half or more of the debt relief in most of the eight countries studied in this book consisted of debt forgiveness as opposed to rescheduling, while forgiveness represented only 15 per cent in Peru. Table 3.1 shows what this signified in relation to outstanding public debt in the preceding year.

Nicaragua, which received a great deal of debt relief, including fairly considerable forgiveness, shows the greatest debt reduction, both in annual average percentages and in per cent of total 1999 debt (see last two columns of Table 3.1). In 1995 and 1996, large sums were forgiven by some bilateral creditors: the former German Democratic Republic in 1995, the former Soviet Union and Mexico in 1996. In 1995, there was also a buyback of private debt. The contribution made by the Paris Club was small, partly because Nicaragua owed relatively little to Club members. Mozambique also received substantial debt relief, but the share of forgiveness was lower than in the case of Nicaragua (Table 2.4). The annual average percentage of public debt that has been forgiven is relatively high (6.1 per cent, Table 3.1), but that was caused primarily by the high percentage in 1990. That figure may not be accurate.[1] As per cent of the 1999 debt, debt reduction in Mozambique was far less than that in Nicaragua.

In the remaining countries, average annual debt reductions were far smaller (between 1.3 and 3.6 per cent). During the 1990s, Bolivia received mostly bilateral debt forgiveness within the Paris Club framework. Multilateral forgiveness started in 1998 and was relatively small. In Zambia, the greatest debt reduction occurred in 1994 as the result of a buyback operation. Uganda's debt was reduced chiefly due to a buyback in 1993 and to multilateral debt relief in 1998. In Tanzania, the slight reduction was due largely to agreements with the Paris Club. Jamaica benefited from debt reduction only at the start of the 1990s, particularly in 1991. In Peru, debt reduction has been slight, and that was mostly taken care of by the Brady operation in 1996, which was not financed by aid funds.

In relation to the high debts and the severe lack of solvency shown by seven of the eight countries in 1990 (Table 2.2 above), the average annual debt reduction in the 1990s was minimal. Debt reduction as per cent of the 1999 debt was also small, with the exception of Nicaragua. That was of course largely influenced by the new loans that the countries received as well as the size of repayments made. Table 3.2 shows that new loans were quite considerable: for almost all countries, the average annual increment

Table 3.1 Debt forgiveness[a] as per cent of total public debt in the preceding year, 1990–1999

	1990	1991	1992	1993	1994	1995	1996	1997	1998	1999	Average	Total[b]
Bolivia	4.9	11.6	2.4	5.4	0.5	2.0	4.1	2.2	0.4	3.0	3.6	55
Jamaica	0.7	8.9	0.7	3.0	0.7	0.0	0.0	0.0	0.0	0.2	1.4	19
Nicaragua	0.0	5.2	0.1	0.0	0.2	23.5	46.8	5.8	0.9	1.5	8.4	122
Peru	0.0	0.0	0.5	0.0	0.0	0.0	10.5	0.0	0.6	0.9	1.3	12
Mozambique	30.4[c]	5.6	0.5	0.8	1.3	6.2	2.5	4.2	0.6	9.0	6.1	60
Tanzania	2.1	3.0	2.7	4.0	1.7	2.3	0.5	5.7	1.2	0.4	2.4	22
Uganda	2.8	0.0	0.6	6.4	0.3	1.4	0.0	0.0	18.1	0.0	3.0	30
Zambia	3.9	2.0	4.9	6.9	13.7	0.1	0.6	0.0	0.0	1.7	3.4	38

Source: Calculated on the basis of World Bank, Global Development Finance CD-ROM, 2002.

Notes
a Defined as the sum of forgiveness on principal and interest due, debt reduction and reduced by funds spent on buybacks.
b The total of all debt forgiveness as per cent of the 1999 public debt.
c The high percentage is due primarily to a debt reduction of US$ 950 million in that year; however, this cannot be traced to any reduction of the debt stock. This inconsistency may be attributable to an inaccuracy or may have originated because a debt had first been revalued and then (partially) forgiven. The facts are not known.

Table 3.2 New loans to government[a] as per cent of public debt in the preceding year, 1990–1999

	1990	1991	1992	1993	1994	1995	1996	1997	1998	1999	Average
Bolivia	8.7	7.7	11.1	8.7	10.0	10.4	8.0	8.8	7.6	6.8	8.8
Jamaica	7.6	10.7	8.5	6.0	3.1	6.8	6.2	10.2	13.4	4.8	7.7
Nicaragua	7.6	3.8	3.1	1.1	3.6	2.9	2.6	11.8	4.8	5.0	4.6
Peru	2.3	3.9	4.1	9.7	3.7	4.1	2.0	7.5	3.3	5.6	4.6
Mozambique	5.4	2.7	4.5	4.0	4.7	4.4	5.4	4.8	4.3	2.2	4.3
Tanzania	5.7	4.8	6.7	4.1	4.4	4.2	3.3	4.1	3.6	4.0	4.5
Uganda	15.8	8.7	11.1	16.8	10.3	8.0	7.4	9.3	5.1	5.0	9.8
Zambia	3.9	7.8	5.8	5.3	6.6	6.8	4.4	5.1	1.2	3.8	5.1

Source: World Bank, Global Development Finance CD-ROM, 2002.

Note

a New foreign loans to government ('Disbursements' on 'public and publicly guaranteed Debt', PPG).

was greater than the average reduction. Only in Nicaragua and Mozambique was the situation reversed. The effect of these new loans on debt sustainability will be discussed in Chapter 4.

Reduction of the flow: debt service

An important argument in favour of debt relief is that it reduces payment obligations for debtor countries, so that they can then use the freed resources for development purposes. The larger part of debt relief received by the eight countries during the 1990s was indeed relief on flows (by means of rescheduling and forgiveness, see Table 2.4), so that a flow reduction can be expected.

In Chapter 1, however, it was already indicated briefly that by no means all debt relief leads to a reduction of actual debt service paid. It does not only depend on the modality of debt relief but also on the type of creditor and on circumstances. More in particular, six factors or circumstances can be distinguished which may prevent debt relief from leading to the actual release of resources:

1   Debt relief (rescheduling or forgiveness) on a debt service flow that has so far not been paid will not reduce the actual payment burden.
2   Debt relief that reduces an outstanding debt (stock reduction), on which no interest or principal repayments were being made, does not lead to lower debt service but frequently to higher actual payments: such agreements routinely require that the remaining, reduced, debt be serviced punctually.
3   Although the rescheduling of payment obligations will reduce debt service in the short term, the shift towards the future means that payments in future years will be higher than they would have been without rescheduling.
4   Debt relief and aid given by one creditor may mean that another creditor can be paid, while that probably would not have happened in the absence of that relief and aid. This is known as 'bailing out'. Total debt service actually paid by the debtor remains the same, but there is a redistribution among the creditors.
5   Debt relief may replace regular development aid and in that case does not supply additional funds to the recipient country.
6   Finally, debt relief may induce a new inflow of loans. On the one hand, debt relief thus has an indirect positive effect on the availability of funds (but that is a stock effect, see Chapter 4); on the other hand, it has a negative flow effect because the total debt service may increase.

As will be discussed below, evidence of all six factors and circumstances has been found for the eight countries. First, the results of some comparative research will be presented, especially on points 4 and 5, the issues of bailing out and of additionality.

Bailing out

The first question is whether debt relief, new aid and loans by a particular group of creditors will lead to payment of the debts of other creditors (bailing out). Chapter 2 concluded that commercial creditors started to withdraw early from debtor countries and that they wrote off their dubious claims before official creditors did so. Nevertheless, in the 1980s, commercial creditors were able to extract more from Latin-American debtor countries than they provided in new loans (Figure 3.1). Between 1983 and 1994, net flows to the region were negative, at the expense of the countries' incomes but also of official creditors. In the peak years of Latin America's debt crisis (1984–1992), private creditors were partly bailed out by their official counterparts.

The net flow of private creditors to Africa was also mostly negative after 1983 (Figure 3.2). After about 1990 that also applied to bilateral creditors. However, the total net inflow of funds to the region remained positive due to the fact that bilateral creditors (who frequently also were donors) started to transfer large sums in the form of grants that replaced

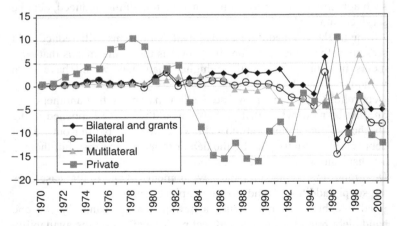

Figure 3.1 Net transfers on debt (new loans minus interest and principal repayment) by type of creditor to Latin America and the Caribbean, 1970–2000, in US$ billions (source: Global Development Finance, 2001).

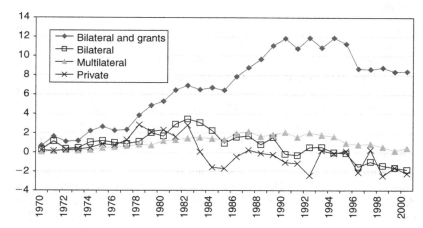

Figure 3.2 Net transfers on debt (new loans minus interest and principal repayment) by type of creditor to Sub-Sahara Africa, 1970–2000, in US$ billions (source: Global Development Finance, 2001.

the loans formerly given. The multilateral flow also remained positive, although far smaller than the bilateral flow. Moreover, debt service to multilateral creditors always had priority: they were preferred creditors. Through their higher priority, the new loans provided by multilateral organizations caused the older debt titles of bilateral creditors to lose value; in addition, several bilateral donors provided grants for the payment of multilateral debt service. It can thus be concluded that, in a way, bilateral debt relief and bilateral grants made it possible for debt service to other groups of creditors [including export credit agencies (ECAs)] to be paid. Once again, it is a case of bailing out but now of private and multilateral creditors and of ECAs by bilateral donors.[2]

In fact, therefore, bilateral donors in the Paris Club contributed in three different ways to the flow of concessional loans by the multilateral institutions: first, by making these concessional loans possible[3]; second, because their own claims lost value and thus required more bilateral debt relief; and third, by taking over debt service to multilateral institutions, whether partially or in full, through the fifth dimension, a Multilateral Debt Fund (MDF) or through contributions to HIPC Trust Funds in the IMF and the World Bank that finance part of multilateral debt forgiveness of the HIPC initiative.

Additionality

Debt relief is additional if the regular aid flow is just as great as in the counterfactual case without debt relief. The issue can be looked at from the perspective of the donor or from that of the recipient country. But establishing this counterfactual is difficult. On the part of the relief *provider*, it can be checked from which budget the debt relief is financed and whether the aid budget would have been greater in the absence of debt relief. It is impossible to do this for all providers collectively, however, because the hypothetical aid budgets in the absence of debt relief are unknown.

Yet most debt relief, even if it does not free resources for the recipient, qualifies as aid, Official Development Assistance (ODA), according to the definition of the Development Assistance Committee (DAC) of the Organization for Economic Cooperation and Development (OECD).[4] This means that to the extent that aid (ODA) budgets are fixed in terms of a certain percentage of gross national product (GNP) – as is the case in the Netherlands and Sweden, for example – debt relief cannot be additional from the donor point of view. However, debt relief from that particular donor can still be additional for an individual debtor country, but in that case aid (and debt relief) to other countries will be reduced. For other donors, debt relief may lead to higher ODA than would otherwise have been the case.

Additionality for an individual recipient implies that the regular aid flow remains the same in the presence of debt relief. It is very difficult to establish the counterfactual aid flow (i.e. in the absence of debt relief) from all donors to this particular country. However, the only thing that matters for a recipient country is whether increased debt relief in a particular year does not reduce the aid flow on that year compared to the preceding year. A negative relation between aid and debt relief over time indicates that the relief has replaced aid; a positive relation or the absence of any link may indicate additionality.

The Global Development Finance (GDF) database, however, also includes debt relief by creditors who do not provide aid. This probably represents half of total debt relief provided during the 1990s, including debt relief (write-offs, buybacks) by private creditors and by bilateral creditors such as the former Soviet Union or other former non-market economies that do not provide aid or have stopped doing so. This form of debt relief is thus always additional.

Some recent studies have econometrically examined the relationship between debt relief and aid for a large group of countries. Ndikumana (2004) finds for the period 1989–2000 no relationship between debt relief and aid. On the aggregate level, 'debt relief' and 'debt forgiveness' in this period did not lead to a reduction in ODA, and individual donors supplying debt forgiveness did not reduce their (other) ODA flows. This points to additionality of debt relief during this period from a donor point of view. As to the recipient side, he finds that for a group of 111 developing countries, there is no relationship between debt forgiven and aid over this period. However, for the period 1997–2000, there is a positive relationship between debt relief and aid in general as well as between debt relief and concessional loans. This means that in this period, debt relief influenced the allocation of ODA among developing countries: countries receiving debt relief also received higher volumes of aid. The author ascribes this effect to the HIPC initiative, but in practice very few countries received HIPC relief before 2001, as most countries only reached the decision point in 2000.[5]

Powell examines additionality of debt relief for 63 International Development Association (IDA)-only countries in the period 1996–2000. Debt relief is defined as 'action related to debt' in the OECD–DAC data and as 'debt reduction or forgiveness' according to the GDF database. Controlling for other variables that may influence aid to a particular country, he finds no evidence of a relationship between debt relief and aid, so there is no significant crowding out of other aid flows in individual recipients of debt relief in this period. Given that global aid budgets did not grow in that period nor were expected to grow in subsequent years, he concludes that there has potentially been divergence of resources from non-HIPCs to HIPCs (Powell 2003).

Flow reduction in the eight countries

Figures 3.3 and 3.4 show that in none of the eight countries did the nominal value of the debt service paid show a clear fall during the 1990s. Peru had a definite rise, while Zambia and to a lesser degree Tanzania experienced heavy fluctuations. In Bolivia, Jamaica and Uganda, the actual debt service paid remained fairly constant, while in Nicaragua (with the exception of the peak in 1991) and Mozambique, the debt service at first rose slightly and then fell slightly. It will now be analysed to what extent the six factors that may prevent debt relief from leading to the freeing of resources (see 'Reduction of the flow: debt service') influenced developments in debt service in the eight countries.

The most extreme case is that of Peru, where debt relief had no effect whatsoever on the flow of debt service payments. Debt relief only cleared away accumulated arrears: the complete net present value of arrears to the IMF (in 1991), paid from aid by bilateral donors, and arrears to private

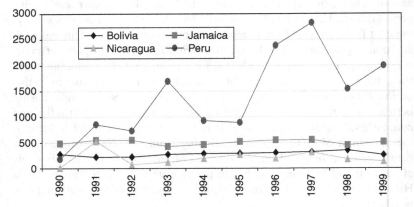

Figure 3.3 Debt service paid on public debt: Bolivia, Jamaica, Nicaragua and Peru, 1990–1999, in US$ millions (source: Global Development Finance).

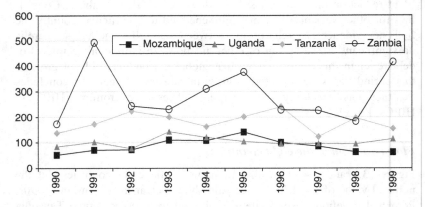

Figure 3.4 Debt service paid on public debt: Mozambique, Uganda, Tanzania and Zambia, 1990–1999, in US$ millions (source: Global Development Finance).

creditors against considerable discount under a Brady agreement in 1996–1997. Debt service increased because Peru entered into many new debts.

In many other countries, too, the majority of debt relief was destined for arrears and for debts that would otherwise not have been paid. In Uganda, Tanzania, Zambia and Nicaragua, arrears were already high in 1990 (see Chapter 2), and there was a strong negative correlation between

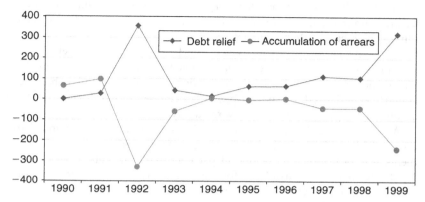

Figure 3.5 Uganda: debt relief and the accumulation of arrears, 1990–1999, in US$ millions (source: Lindner (2003a), based on Global Development Finance data).

debt relief and the accumulation of arrears. Figure 3.5 illustrates this inverse relationship for Uganda: a large amount of debt relief coincided with, and thus was used for, a great reduction of arrears. Similar graphs could be presented for Nicaragua, Tanzania and Zambia.

Debt relief provided by the Paris Club to Nicaragua, Mozambique, Uganda, Tanzania and Zambia during the first half of the decade included above all the restructuring and forgiving of arrears. Prior to the agreements, the creditors in question had not been paid. Around the mid-1990s, however, the arrears were smaller, and these countries started to service their debt service due to the Paris Club members. From then on, it can be said that debt relief by the Paris Club also reduced actual payments to some extent.

Debt relief received from private creditors and from bilateral creditors who did not belong to the Paris Club (e.g. Russia) frequently increased actual debt service. These other forms of debt relief played an important part in Nicaragua's total debt relief, but they also occurred in Zambia, Uganda, Mozambique and Tanzania. Paris Club agreements in the 1980s and at the start of the 1990s sometimes caused debt service to increase later in that decade. The sole form of debt relief that unequivocally freed resources for the governments of these four countries was that of bilateral takeover of multilateral debt obligations (because the latter were always paid). However, such modes of debt relief often replaced other forms of macro-economic support or programme aid and thus did not always provide the recipient government with additional funds.

In Bolivia, debt service to the Paris Club members was paid throughout the 1990s. This implied that debt forgiveness and rescheduling provided by the Club reduced actual debt service. Jamaica was given only rescheduling, which caused debt payments later in the decade to increase. Nevertheless, Jamaica is the country where the flow effect of debt relief was probably the greatest: it allowed the country to spread payments throughout the decade. They were lower in the first half of the decade when the country experienced balance-of-payments problems and higher in the second half when these problems were largely over.

All in all, the flow effect of debt relief was greatest in Jamaica and also considerable in Bolivia. In the other countries, the effect on actual payments was probably (far) below 50 per cent, while in Peru it was zero. Most information was available for Nicaragua, where only 5 per cent of total debt relief received in the 1990s proved to have led to an actual reduction of the debt service.

Additionality in the eight countries

In all eight countries, debt relief was additional to aid from the perspective of the recipient country: in general, no negative correlation existed between debt relief and aid. An exception must be made for one modality of debt relief, namely bilateral relief on multilateral debt service, through the fifth dimension or an MDF. This frequently replaced other forms of macro-economic support (or programme aid): balance of payments or budget support and was in those cases not additional for the recipient.

This conclusion is broadly in line with those of the econometric studies on the subject cited above. But again, additionality on the individual recipient level does not imply that the donors involved made debt relief available in addition to what they would have spent on aid loans and grants without debt relief. The additionality for these eight debtors may very well have been achieved by withdrawing the funds from destinations that they would otherwise have had, e.g. as aid flows towards less-indebted countries. This is certainly the case for a creditor/donor such as the Netherlands, where most debt relief is financed from a fixed [in terms of gross domestic product (GDP)] aid budget. At the same time, a large part of debt relief during the 1990s was provided by creditors who are not donors (anymore): private creditors or bilateral creditors such as the former Soviet Union or other former non-market economies that do not provide aid or have stopped doing so. Debt relief from these creditors was always additional.

Bailing out in the eight countries

In all eight countries, payments to multilateral institutions always took priority over payments to other groups of creditors. A few countries (Nicaragua, Peru and Zambia) got into arrears in the 1980s, but these had been cleared by the start of the 1990s (with the help of bilateral grants and bridging loans); since then, the most important multilateral creditors (i.e. the IMF, the World Bank and the Inter-American Development Bank) have always been paid. This is shown by the fact that in almost all countries, the share of multilateral *debt service* in total debt service was higher than the multilateral share of *debt* (Figure 3.6). This was notwithstanding the fact that in six of the eight countries (the exceptions being the middle-income countries Jamaica and Peru), most multilateral debt is concessional and thus carries a lower debt service burden.[6] Only in Uganda, where the share of multilateral creditors in the total debt is also the highest (almost 70 per cent) and where virtually 100 per cent of the outstanding multilateral debt throughout the decade was concessional, the share of the multilaterals in the outstanding debt was greater than their share in the debt service, even though the latter still exceeded 50 per cent. Multilateral debt service was also 50 per cent or more in Bolivia, Nicaragua, Tanzania and

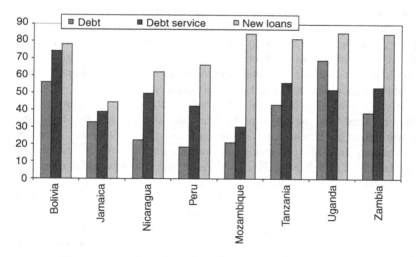

Figure 3.6 Share of multilateral creditors in the total public debt, debt service and new loans to the government (source: Global Development Finance, 2002).* of the eight countries, 1990–1999, in per cent

Note
This concerns the multilateral share in 'public and publicly guaranteed debt' (PPG): i.e. in 'Debt Outstanding and Disbursed' (DOD), 'total debt service' (TDS) and 'Disbursements' (DIS) respectively.

Zambia, i.e. in five of the six HIPCs investigated. The HIPC initiative, under which multilateral institutions for the first time waived part of the debt service to themselves, could be expected to be of great significance for this group of countries.

Figure 3.6 also shows that the share of multilateral creditors in new loans to all eight countries is very considerable. In the four African countries, it amounted to over 80 per cent and was not much less in Bolivia. Even in middle-income Peru, multilaterals were responsible for three-fifths of the increase in public debt during the 1990s. Only in Jamaica was the share of multilateral new loans less than 50 per cent. As a rule, concessional multilateral loans have a grace period of ten years (in the case of IMF five years). It is thus no surprise that debt problems have continued in HIPCs in the present decade, making the new Multilateral Debt Relief Initiative (MDRI) necessary.

Implementation of policy conditions

Implementation of IMF programmes in general

Creditors united in the Paris Club hoped to achieve various objectives with their demand that countries sign an agreement with the IMF regarding structural adjustment. First, it was thought that it would lead to better policy-making, thus improving the balance of payments position and the future repayment of debts. Second, it was expected that an IMF agreement would have a catalysing effect on the inflow of new loans and grants, thus enabling the country to solve its payment problems.

Collier *et al.* (1997) have pointed out that these two functions, i.e. on the one hand, 'buying' good policy (ex ante) and, on the other hand, the rewarding of good behaviour (ex post) are logically inconsistent. Research has shown that IMF agreements do not cause an inflow of new private capital (Bird and Rowlands 2000). As a rule, an agreement regarding structural adjustment leads to programme aid by bilateral donors and, of course, also to programme aid by the multilaterals. The catalysing effect thus seems to apply only to official creditors and donors.

The implementation of the policy conditions was also uninspiring. Frequently, structural adjustment programmes were not carried out as agreed. In 24 of the 30 IMF Extended Fund Facilities (EFF), re-negotiations were necessary, or the programme was discontinued (Haggard 1985). Out of 25 Enhanced Structural Adjustment Facility (ESAF) programmes examined, only five were completed according to plan; in 14 cases, the period of implementation had to be extended, and two were discontinued (Killick 1995).

Dreher (2006) provides an excellent summary of the literature on compliance with IMF conditions. This shows that non-compliance has been a continuous problem in IMF programmes, whether measured by actual compliance with particular conditions, interruptions of programmes or the non-drawing of all committed resources. According to this last measure, the annual average of the Stand-by and EFF programmes over the period 1980–1999 where at least 25 per cent of resources remained undrawn at programme completion was 43 per cent. He also looked at the share of committed resources per year that was actually purchased in these programmes. In that case, the annual average share of programmes where at least 25 per cent of resources remained undrawn was even higher, namely 65 per cent (Dreher 2006). Another indicator for the limited effectiveness of the IMF policy conditions is the extent of recidivism, which is especially high among low-income countries (Bird 2001; Easterly 2002; Sachs 2002).

Research into World Bank programmes shows roughly the same results as regards implementation of policy conditions (Mosley *et al.* 1991; Killick *et al.* 1998). Adjustment measures that were actually carried out had mostly already been intended by the country in question; sometimes, measures were only 'cosmetically' implemented, or the government simultaneously took other measures that undid the intended effects.

In general, it seems that mostly domestic political factors determine which policy changes are implemented and which are not. Factors that the World Bank can influence, e.g. the number of preconditions, preparation and monitoring of the programme, have little effect in comparison (Dollar and Svensson 2000). Another study of the implementation of IMF and World Bank programmes also concluded that domestic political factors in particular determine whether reforms will be implemented (Dijkstra 2002). If the recipient country is under heavy pressure to reach an agreement with IMF and World Bank, perhaps due to heavy indebtedness, then such an agreement will almost always come about. Similar pressure may sometimes cause reforms to be implemented that were not actually intended. Agreed measures will above all be implemented if:

1   donor and recipient have similar objectives
2   the political costs of implementation are not too high.

Implementation is also encouraged if the aid that accompanies the agreement can be used to attain target figures, e.g. with regard to public deficits, or to compensate important political groups that suffer loss as a result of the reforms.

Another reason why adjustment programmes are implemented so inadequately is that sanctions on non-compliance, e.g. the stopping of aid, are

seldom effective (Killick *et al.* 1998). Donors have many varying objectives: they want to continue to help heavily indebted countries and also
those that are very poor and thus are in great need of aid. On the assump-
tion that the prescribed reforms represent 'good policy', and that the
country will become more indebted and poorer if the reforms are not
implemented, this could lead to countries with poor policies receiving
more aid: i.e. adverse selection. If a donor decides to discontinue aid, other
donors often take its place. The lack of donor co-ordination reduces the
effectiveness of possible sanctions. Moreover, aid is seldom halted in
countries with high economic growth because that would detract from the
credibility of donors (Mosley 1996).

Finally, countries that are heavily indebted to international financial
institutions will always be able to obtain a new IMF agreement and thus a
new loan. Programmes may be interrupted due to non-compliance, but
negotiations will immediately start on a new programme. The IMF has an
interest in a new programme because that will bring in World Bank adjustment loans and bilateral programme aid (White and Dijkstra 2003). This
freely spendable money can be used for payment of earlier IMF and World
Bank loans.

Several studies have already shown that HIPCs, and especially countries with high multilateral debts, receive more aid (Marchesi and Missale
2004). They observe not only 'defensive lending' but also 'defensive
granting': countries with high multilateral debts receive more grants than
other low-income countries. Birdsall *et al.* (2003) report not only that
countries with high multilateral debts received more aid, but that aid is
also going to countries with worse policies. Easterly (2002: 1692) finds
that HIPCs received more financing from the IMF and the World Bank
over the period 1979–1997 than other low-income countries, despite their
worse policies. This is clear evidence of adverse selection. It can be considered the result of the mechanism that repayment of the debts to the multilateral institutions depends on a flow of freely spendable resources (i.e.
programme aid) from both multilateral and bilateral donors. This flow is
usually linked (conditioned) to an agreement with the IMF. Figure 3.7 provides more evidence of this mechanism, showing that although programme aid declined during the 1990s, this decline was much smaller for
the HIPCs than for the non-HIPCs.

The conclusion that most studies draw from the defective implementation of policy conditions is that donors would do better to evaluate a
country retrospectively rather than to set prior conditions (Collier *et al.*
1997; World Bank 1998; Dreher 2006). Another reason for some caution
in drawing up policy conditions is that there are often several viable
alternative policies that may be followed and that the policy prescribed by

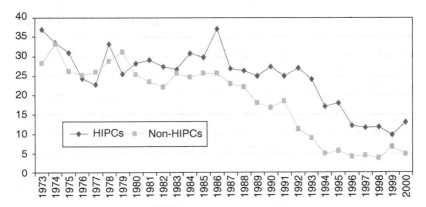

Figure 3.7 Share of programme aid in total aid, 1973–2000, in per cent (source: Own elaboration on the basis of OECD, International Development Statistics CD-ROM, 2002).

the donors has not always promoted the welfare of the country (Stiglitz 1998; Easterly 2006).

Implementation of IMF and World Bank programmes in the eight countries

IMF agreements with the eight countries on which this study is focused, specified targets for financial deficits and growth of the money supply. Furthermore, and often in conjuncture with the World Bank, conditions were set regarding the trade liberalization, the privatization of state industries (in particular public utilities and state banks), the liberalization of the financial sector and the reforms of the public sector. The latter concerned reducing its size and making it more efficient but also decentralization and improvement of financial management and accountability. From the mid-1990s onwards, conditions were also introduced for social policies, e.g. that countries should set up a Social Fund (Peru, Jamaica), that they should reform their pension system (Bolivia) or that a certain percentage of government expenditure should be allocated to the social sectors (Zambia). In countries with an MDF, requirements regarding social policy often started with the MDF and concerned usage of the countervalue of debt relief.

The eight countries investigated in this study show none too favourable a picture as regards implementation of IMF and World Bank agreements. There are considerable variations, however. Since 1993, Bolivia, Mozambique and Uganda have always been on track with the IMF, while

Tanzania has had a good track record since 1996. However, these countries have often been slow in implementing reforms required by the World Bank, and donors are far from being satisfied with policies to achieve control of corruption, decentralization and increased transparency of public expenditure management.

Since 1991, Zambia has carried out numerous reforms at a fast pace, but it has been late in privatizing state industries, particularly the state copper mines. This did not occur until 2000, which meant many years of major losses for the state and thus caused problems in reaching the IMF target for the public deficit. Zambia has often been depicted as a country with poor policies during the 1990s (World Bank 1998; Dollar *et al.* 2001). On average, however, it was no slower in introducing reforms than Uganda for example and was quicker in many respects after 1991. Nevertheless, and possibly because of this, the economy continued to stagnate. In Uganda, until 1992, high economic growth caused a blind eye to be turned to many policy shortcomings; also after 1992, requirements regarding the speed of reforms were far lower than elsewhere (Dijkstra and Van Donge 2001).

Nicaragua implemented all IMF programmes during their first year only, and that was mainly achieved due to the inflow of programme aid in those years. Subsequently, the country invariably went off track, although not always officially.[7] Other reforms, too, were implemented far slower than required, and after 1996, relations with donors worsened because of issues related to good governance. Jamaica usually implemented IMF programmes according to the letter but not the spirit. In Peru, in 1991, the new liberal government implemented all required stabilization, privatization and liberalization measures because these were in complete agreement with its own targets. Even the creation of a Social Fund in 1993 did not represent a problem since President Fujimori was able to utilize it as a political tool. When Peru was required to confront the drugs trade, however, IMF conditions were not implemented. Later, it appeared that high ranking government officials were themselves involved in the trade.

Towards the end of the 1990s, it became increasingly important, particularly for the six HIPCs in the group, that IMF requirements be satisfied because the countries were seriously in need of debt relief. Most of them therefore did at least that which was considered minimally necessary. Bolivia, Mozambique, Tanzania, Uganda and Zambia took care to meet the IMF targets, and all six drew up a Poverty Reduction Strategy Paper (PRSP). Although they needed the HIPC qualification and were thus dependent on donors, conversely, the latter were also dependent on the governments of the countries involved.

By the end of the decade, Mozambique, Tanzania and Uganda can be characterized as 'post-conditionality regimes' (Harrison 2001), whereby donors are keen to be able to continue to give aid and thus to maintain the image of a country that performs well. This image is based on the relatively high economic growth in those countries: donors need such success stories. On the one hand, governments of the recipient countries are prepared to satisfy the wishes of the donors; on the other hand, donors will be less severe if they observe slippage in the developing country. In practice, this occurs primarily in matters related to good governance. In HIPCs, yet another factor augmented this mutual dependency, namely pressure by the international community and particularly by international non-governmental organizations (NGOs) to admit as many countries as possible to the HIPC initiative. This encouraged donor inclination to ignore non-compliance with certain agreements or to back-pedal on certain demands. They admitted countries to the HIPC initiative even though their poverty strategy was insufficiently elaborated[8] and tended to tolerate corruption and other forms of bad governance.

Conclusions

Debt relief efforts made by the international community have so far led to only a slight actual reduction of the debt stock. This is because the volume of debt relief has generally not been large in relation to outstanding debt and also because a large part of received debt relief only restructured debt and did not cancel it. With the exception of Nicaragua and Mozambique, the annual accretion of new debt in the countries investigated was greater than annual debt relief.

Notwithstanding the large share of rescheduling and forgiveness of flows in the total debt relief, debt relief had little effect on the flow of actual payments, the debt service. In this respect, it was thus not efficient. Reduction of a debt stock on which nothing had so far been repaid, in fact often caused actual debt service payments to increase. In none of the eight countries did actual debt payments decrease in the 1990s, partly due to the increase in new loans.

In general, debt relief in the 1990s for the eight countries was additional to regular aid. On the one hand, it came partly from creditors that were not donors (e.g. private banks and former socialist countries); on the other hand, debt relief from donors/creditors was probably financed partly at the expense of aid to *other*, less-indebted countries. The amounts involved in takeover of multilateral obligations by bilateral donors were usually not additional for recipient countries because these monies often replaced other forms of programme aid. At the same time, this modality of debt relief is the only one that unambiguously frees resources for the debtor country because debt service to multilateral institutions was always paid.

During the 1980s, private creditors were bailed out by official lenders. This continued in the 1990s, but bilateral donors then also bailed out multilateral creditors on a large scale. Bilateral donors were in a sense contributing in three different ways to the financing of the concessional loans from the multilateral institutions: first, by making the loans possible through subsidies and periodical 'replenishments'; second, by agreeing with the preferential status of the loans, thus reducing the value of their own claims; and finally, by giving extra aid to the debtors concerned, including debt relief on (or the takeover of) multilateral claims. This cannot be an efficient use of aid money. Such bilateral financing and bailout enabled multilateral creditors to continue to provide imprudent loans for longer than would have been feasible if they had been saddled with the consequences of their own lending policy. Protection against part of those consequences by bilateral donors created *moral hazard* on the part of the institutions concerned. Of the new loans that governments of the six HIPCs took up in the 1990s, roughly 80 per cent were granted by multilateral institutions (only Nicaragua had rather less, with approximately 60 per cent).

In general, the prior setting of policy conditions for economic reform proved effective if the government concerned was itself already convinced of the correctness of the policies, which makes such conditionality not really necessary. To hold out the prospect of debt relief makes little difference. Conditions regarding good governance were seldom implemented. In that respect, too, debt relief has not been very efficient.

By entering into new adjustment agreements notwithstanding the deficient implementation of policy conditions, multilateral institutions have, as it were, given the debtor countries their seal of approval. This led to new programme aid being provided by bilateral donors with which old debts to multilaterals could be repaid. The IMF and, to a lesser degree, the World Bank were simultaneously 'gatekeepers' for concessional funds and, as creditors, also stakeholders in those funds. This undesirable conflict of interest has helped to maintain the cycle of new loans, aid and debt relief.

4 The effectiveness of debt relief

In this chapter, the effectiveness of debt relief in the 1990s is analysed by comparing outputs with outcomes. A primary aspect of effectiveness is the increase of debt sustainability. It is therefore investigated whether the debt burden has been reduced, i.e. whether the countries have acquired greater liquidity and have become more solvent during the 1990s. Debt sustainability can be improved by reducing the debt stock or the debt service, but also by economic growth or export growth (the denominators of the debt burden indicators). The analysis attempts to establish to what extent eventual improvements are due to debt relief. This chapter also analyses whether debt relief has had stock and flow effects on economic growth (and poverty reduction). A stock effect occurs if a debt stock reduction leads to improved creditworthiness thus enabling the attraction of new foreign capital and if domestic investments increase. There is evidence of a flow effect if additional funds that result from debt relief lead to increased imports and have positive effects on the government budget. Ultimately, social indicators may thus be improved.

These three aspects of effectiveness are examined first at an aggregate level for the regions of Latin America and Africa and subsequently for the eight countries. This chapter ends with a discussion of long-term sustainability of debts in the eight countries.

Effectiveness of debt relief in Latin America and Africa

Since 1988, the external debt burden has been sustainable for the average Latin-American country (see Figure 4.1). The debt/gross national product (GNP) ratio reached its highest value in 1987 but then began to fall to about 45 per cent in 1990; thereafter, it remained fairly steady until the end of the decade. The implication is that most countries had again become solvent. Debt itself actually only fell between 1988 and 1990 and increased again thereafter. Debt reductions were primarily achieved by amortizations paid by the countries themselves, but debt forgiveness also played a role in 1988–1990. The improved debt sustainability in the 1990s was chiefly due to increased GNP.

The debt service/export ratio in Latin America was above 35 per cent between 1978 and 1988, falling to 24 per cent in 1991 (Figure 4.2). In absolute terms, debt service decreased between 1988 and 1991 (possibly due to the fall in nominal debt stock in the same period), and exports increased even more. In the second half of the 1990s, in particular, the debt service/export ratio again rose, as the result of two developments. First, arrears fell rapidly after 1991, from roughly US$50 billion in 1991 to about US$10 billion in 1996; in the 1990s, as a result, Latin America paid almost all its debt obligations.[1] Second, Latin America regained access to private capital, which naturally also entailed an increase in payment obligations. Altogether, Latin-American debt seems to be sustainable, but the liquidity position remains vulnerable. Export growth lagged behind general economic development, and the countries continue to depend heavily on the inflow of foreign capital.

It is important here to consider the role that debt relief played in the increase of economic growth, i.e. in improving the debt's sustainability by increasing its denominator. Were there stock or flow effects? Literature on the Brady deals is fairly unanimous in concluding that these agreements improved the countries' creditworthiness, measured by an increase in secondary market prices and/or by a new inflow of private capital (Boehmer and Megginson 1990; Acharya and Diwan 1993; Dooley *et al.* 1994; Bowe and Dean 1997). Thus, there was a stock effect.[2] The nature of the inflow changed: in the first half of the 1990s, in particular, portfolio equity

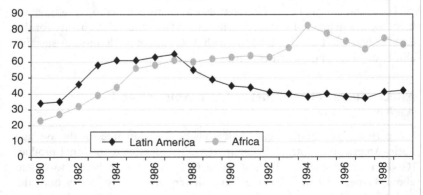

Figure 4.1 Debt/GNP ratio in Latin America and Africa, 1980–1999, in per cent (source: World Bank, Global Development Finance, 2001).

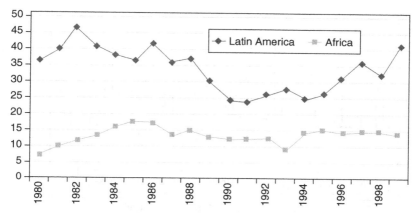

Figure 4.2 Debt service/export ratio in Latin America and Africa, 1980–1999, in per cent (source: World Bank, Global Development Finance, 2001).

flows took the place of bank loans; later, however, net loans again increased. Foreign investments also grew during the 1990s.

In the countries where this has been investigated, there also proved to be a positive effect on investment. A lower outstanding debt reduces volatility in debt repayments and thus the uncertainty regarding future payments. This proved more important than a reduction in the size of the debt service. Reduced uncertainty over possible balance-of-payments crises caused domestic interest rates to fall (Claessens *et al.* 1994). In Argentina too, the effect that debt relief had on interest rates and thereby on private investment proved more significant than the direct flow effect of debt relief on public investment (Morisset 1991).

In Latin America, flow effects of debt relief were barely visible. On the one hand, arrears were considerable, so that restructuring and debt forgiveness only replaced accumulated arrears. On the other hand, the new inflow gave rise to higher debt service. In Latin America, therefore, the stock effects of debt relief, particularly on investment and creditworthiness, seem to have been more important than the flow effects.

In 1987, the debt/GNP ratio reached the 60 per cent level in Africa, but even after that the debt burden continued to increase (Figure 4.1). On average, African countries were still far from solvent by 1999. Debt itself continued to increase until 1995, as did the arrears which amounted to over US$60 billion in 1995, 1996 and 1998 – higher than they have ever been in Latin America.

In Africa, debt service has never been very large, remaining in most

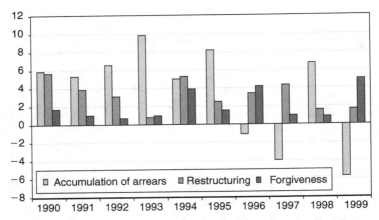

Figure 4.3 Africa: accumulation of arrears (Net year-to-year accumulation, i.e. new arrears minus old arrears that have been paid or forgiven), restructuring and forgiveness of debt service (Only of debt service, i.e. excluding reductions in the debt stock). 1990–1999, in US$ billions (source: Calculated on the basis of World Bank: Global Development Finance, 2002 CD-ROM).

years just under 15 per cent of exports (Figure 4.2). In nominal terms, it did increase slightly during the 1990s. Figure 4.3 shows that, up to and including 1995, the increase in arrears played a role in moderating actual debt service. In 1993 alone, arrears increased by US$10 billion! The volumes involved in restructuring of debt service were significant throughout the period, while debt forgiveness became more important in the second half of the 1990s.

With such massive arrears, debt relief can hardly have a flow effect. Africa received huge amounts in grants, however, so that the net flow of resources remained positive both in the 1980s and in the 1990s (Figure 3.2 above). As mentioned before, however, the larger portion of those grants was project-tied and could thus not be used for the repayment of debts.

In view of the continuing high indebtedness and substantial arrears, stock effects in Africa are also unlikely. In practice, investment remained at the low level of around 16–17 per cent of gross domestic product (GDP), a few percentage points lower even than in the 1980s. Private capital flows towards Africa also remained negative in the 1990s. Since there are few effective stock exchanges in Africa and as many countries have not yet liberalized their capital accounts, possibilities for portfolio investment are limited. There is a great potential for returning flight capital, however. On average, Africans seem to keep a great deal of capital outside the region, namely 40 per cent of their total wealth.[3] Econometric estimates show that a reduction of the debt/GNP ratio could cause flight capital to return (Collier *et al.* 2001). Given the negative net private capital flow, this has apparently not yet taken place. The only capital flow towards Africa that is positive and which also increased in the 1990s is that of foreign direct investment.

Debt sustainability in the eight countries

Solvency

Debt relief may improve the solvency of a country if it leads to a reduction of the debt stock or if it has indirect effects on the denominators of the solvency ratios, GNP and exports. In Table 3.1 above, it was shown that debt stocks were hardly reduced as a result of debt relief. Nevertheless, in most of the eight countries, the debt/GNP ratio improved during the 1990s (Figure 4.4). Zambia is the exception, while Peru, Mozambique and Uganda showed only a slight fall. Nicaragua, Jamaica and Tanzania showed the greatest decrease. In Jamaica, the debt/GNP ratio dropped to less than 60 per cent, in Bolivia, it fell to that level, and it was already less than 60 per cent in Peru and Uganda. Nicaragua, Mozambique, Tanzania and Zambia, according to this indicator, are still far from being solvent.

The strong fall in Nicaragua was due particularly to the large reduction of outstanding debt (Table 3.1 above). Jamaica has received little debt relief but has itself repaid many of its debts. Bolivia and Peru have also made considerable repayments, but on the other hand, they have taken on many new debts. The latter also applies to Uganda and Mozambique. In Zambia, the increase in the debt/GNP ratio is due particularly to lagging economic growth. Nominal GNP in US dollars in 1999 was even 2 per cent lower than in 1990.

Zambia is also the only country where the debt/export ratio rose during the 1990s (Figure 4.5): its exports fell substantially (by 30 per cent between 1990 and 1999). Jamaica was already in the most favourable position as regards the debt/export ratio in 1990 and has further improved in the meantime. Its exports have risen considerably. Once again, Nicaragua shows the greatest improvement, influenced by both debt relief and export growth. In all countries except Jamaica (thus, surprisingly enough also in Peru), the debt/export ratio was still over 250 per cent in 1999; in Mozambique, the 1999 debt was even tenfold the value of exports. According to this indicator, and despite the debt relief provided, debts were still unsustainable in all countries but Jamaica.

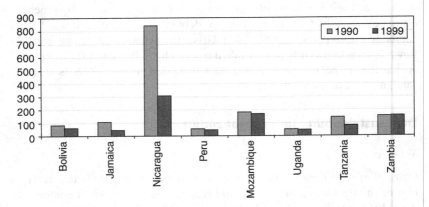

Figure 4.4 Debt/GNP ratios in the eight countries, 1990 and 1999, in per cent (source: World Bank, Global Development Finance, 2002.

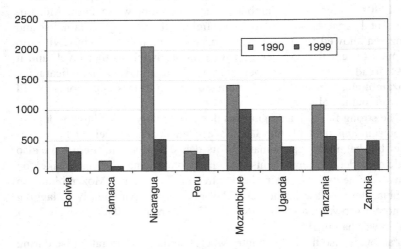

Figure 4.5 Debt/export ratios in the eight countries, 1990 and 1999, in per cent (source: World Bank, Global Development Finance, 2002).

Liquidity

Liquidity indicators include the ratio between debt service and exports, between interest payments and exports and between arrears and debt stock.[4] Debt relief may improve the liquidity position of debtor countries by reducing the flow of payments but also by reducing outstanding debt stock. Given the conclusions of Chapter 3 that the latter was slight, and that only Bolivia and Jamaica experienced any flow reduction as a result of debt relief, much effect on the liquidity position is not to be expected.

In three countries (Nicaragua, Peru and Zambia), the debt service/export ratio has risen, i.e. worsened. These are the countries that were in arrears with the International Financial Institutions (IFIs) in 1990. An important cause of their rising debt service is therefore that in 1991, they started to repay all their obligations to the IFIs. Peru and Zambia were in an unenviable position in 1999 – the debt service/export ratio was over 40 per cent in both countries, while the interest payment/export ratio was at or above the critical value of 15 per cent: 18 per cent in Peru and 15 per cent in Zambia. In Peru, this is due above all to new loans, including those to the private sector; in Zambia, the critical liquidity situation is caused mostly by lagging exports. In 1999, Uganda and Bolivia had already benefited from HIPC 1, but their debt service was still high when compared to exports (22 and 29 per cent, respectively). In 1999, however, these two countries had almost no payment arrears. This was also the case in Mozambique, where debt service was just under 20 per cent of exports. Nicaragua and Tanzania paid only 16 per cent of their exports on debt service, but they still had considerable arrears in 1999 (see Figures 4.6 and 4.7 below).

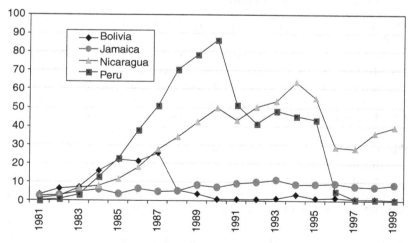

Figure 4.6 Arrears in per cent of long-term debt in Bolivia, Jamaica, Nicaragua and Peru, 1981–1999 (source: Calculated on the basis of World Bank, Global Development Finance, 2002).

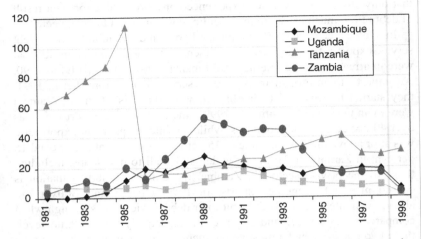

Figure 4.7 Arrears in per cent of long-term debt in Mozambique, Tanzania, Uganda and Zambia, 1981–1999 (source: Calculated on the basis of World Bank, Global Development Finance, 2002).

Stock effect in the eight countries

The question now is whether the (slight) reduction of debt stocks as a result of debt relief has reduced debt overhang in the eight countries and thus had a positive effect on new inflows of capital and on investments. As described in Chapter 1, a reduction of debt overhang can be established by examining the stock of arrears with respect to total outstanding debt and the ratio of debt service paid/debt service due. The first of these should fall, the other rise. If arrears have diminished and if the country services the major part of its obligations, there may be stock effects on creditworthiness, i.e. the inflow of new private capital[5] and an increase of domestic investment.

An indicator of creditworthiness can possibly be derived from scores awarded to countries by established credit rating agencies, such as Moody's and Standard & Poor. Most African countries and some in Latin America, however, are not listed by these institutions. Another agency that evaluates many poor and middle-income countries is Euromoney, whose credit ratings prove to be determined by four factors: the ratio between international reserves and imports, the balance on current account of the balance of payments, the growth of GDP and inflation. Debt ratios do not seem to play a role in their assessments (Ul Haque *et al.* 1999). This indicator is thus of less significance for the present purpose.

With regard to the inflow of capital, the net flows of new loans have been investigated, particularly those of private creditors, as well as net portfolio equity flows and foreign direct investment.[6] As regards the second aspect of the stock effect, i.e. the increase of domestic investment, the ratio between investment and GDP has been investigated. In both cases, it is also analysed whether eventual increases are related to debt relief.

Reduction of the debt overhang

Bolivia had practically no arrears throughout the 1990s (Figure 4.6). In Jamaica and Uganda, they represented only 10 per cent of total debt and remained roughly at that level during the decade (a rise to 20 per cent in 1992 for Uganda, but a fall thereafter). Peru, Nicaragua, Tanzania, Mozambique and Zambia show major arrears in 1990 (Figures 4.6 and 4.7).

Peru reduced its arrears to zero in two stages during the 1990s: first, through a support group of bilateral donors who cleared arrears to the IFIs; second, through a self-financed Brady agreement. Zambia's and Nicaragua's arrears showed a fall, but they remained very high, especially Nicaragua's. Although that country received more debt forgiveness in comparison to others (Table 3.1), this was apparently by no means sufficient to eliminate the debt overhang. Tanzania was not even given sufficient debt forgiveness to enable it to reduce its arrears, which rose during the 1990s. In Mozambique, arrears represented about 20 per cent of total debt over the entire decade. In sum, debt relief in the 1990s appears to have been particularly effective in getting rid of Peru's debt overhang. Arrears were reduced to some extent in Nicaragua and Zambia; other countries showed little change, while in Tanzania, the situation just worsened.

Above it was concluded that the creditworthiness of the average Latin-American country improved during the 1990s. This is also evident from the ratio between debt service paid and due, which climbed to above 90 per cent in 1997–1999 (Table 4.1). In Africa, on the other hand, the ratio even fell during the decade. In this respect, Bolivia and Peru were average Latin-American countries, the ratio increasing to reach more than 90 per cent. This enabled the two to become creditworthy. In Jamaica, the ratio is rather lower, with about 70 per cent. That the ratio is not higher here is entirely due to old arrears outstanding, as the country received no debt relief or restructuring after 1995. Jamaica is therefore probably creditworthy.

In the other countries, the ratio of debt service paid to debt service due

Table 4.1 Ratio of debt service paid[a] to debt service due[b] in Latin America, in Africa and in the eight countries, 1989–1999, in per cent

	1989	1990	1991	1992	1993	1994	1995	1996	1997	1998	1999
Latin America	56	45	42	46	54	59	72	83	92	93	95
Africa	23	24	21	19	13	16	18	18	20	18	17
Bolivia	22	54	36	57	60	69	54	37	53	91	90
Jamaica	62	60	48	58	47	58	62	69	74	69	69
Nicaragua	0	0	9	2	3	3	4	7	16	10	7
Peru	4	4	8	11	24	11	11	36	79	82	97
Mozambique	7	5	6	6	10	9	8	8	6	6	12
Tanzania	13	11	11	11	9	8	8	10	6	11	9
Uganda	46	29	27	20	32	33	31	37	38	15	72
Zambia	8	6	20	12	13	16	73	19	20	17	45

Source: Calculated on the basis of World Bank, Global Development Finance, 2002.

Notes

a Total debt service (TDS) paid on all foreign debt.
b Total of (1) debt service paid, (2) forgiveness of interest and principal obligations due, (3) restructuring of debt service, and (4) the arrears stock.

is much lower but fluctuates considerably from year to year. In 1999, it was over 70 per cent for Uganda, due particularly to the reduction in arrears in that year. Debt service paid showed hardly any increase. In 1998, the ratio was only 15 per cent, principally due to substantial forgiveness of interest payments in that year. In 1995, paid debt service was exceptionally high in Zambia, partly reflected in a lowering of its arrears (Figure 4.7): this explains the 73 per cent ratio in that year. In 1999, there was again evidence of increased debt service payment, combined with a reduction of arrears. Nicaragua, Mozambique and Tanzania mostly paid only about 10 per cent of what they owed, and there was no evidence of any rising trend during the decade. A major part of debt obligations were restructured each year or were simply not paid. In all probability, therefore, these five countries are not creditworthy in the view of the private sector.

Creditworthiness

The primary indicator for the inflow of new foreign capital is the total of net loans. These increased in Bolivia and Peru and slightly in Mozambique if 1990–1994 is compared with 1995–1999 (Figure 4.8). As shown in Chapter 3, however, the major part of new loans, especially to the government, came from multilateral banks (with the exception of Jamaica). In

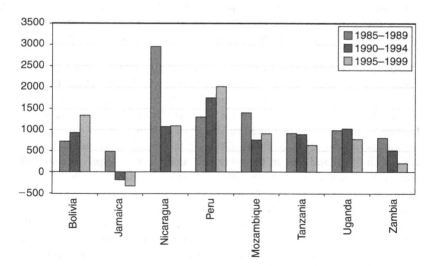

Figure 4.8 Net flows on long-term debt (New long-term loans minus repayments) to the eight countries, 1985–1999, totals per period, in US$ millions (source: World Bank, Global Development Finance, 2002).

five of the eight countries, multilateral loans formed more than three-quarters of the total volume of (gross) new loans (disbursements) to the government (see Figure 3.6). But this says little about creditworthiness in general given that the multilaterals are preferred creditors. Net private loans to governments are negative everywhere, again with the exception of Jamaica. In this country, *total net loans* became even negative in the second part of the decade, primarily because of substantial amortization on official loans: the earlier rescheduling of debt service made considerable debt payments necessary.

It seems that most governments continued to be creditworthy for the IFIs but not for the private sector. In Tanzania, Uganda and Zambia, the net inflow of official capital also decreased during the 1990s.

Bolivia and Peru show a large increase in loans to the private sector, thus confirming the creditworthiness of these countries. In Bolivia, the flow increased from an average of minus US$2 million in the first half of the 1990s to about US$81 million in the second half. In Peru, they rose from an annual average of US$143 million to US$535 million. In 1999, private debt represented a quarter of Peru's total long-term debt. The other countries showed only a slight increase (Jamaica, Nicaragua, Zambia, Mozambique and Uganda, in order of declining increase) or a small decrease (Tanzania).

Another inflow that may indicate improved creditworthiness is that of portfolio investment (portfolio equity flows). Peru is the only country where this form of capital inflow occurs. Since 1993, when the capital account was liberalized, the net inflow has fluctuated between US$0.3 and US$2.7 billion per annum.

Foreign direct investment has increased in all eight countries (Figure 4.9). In 1985–1989, there was hardly any such inflow other than in Zambia. In 1990–1994, inflows started to increase, and grew strongly during the second half of the decade, particularly in Bolivia where many foreign investments were linked to the privatization process – or capitalization as it was there known.[7] Other investors were attracted by the extraction of oil and gas. In the other seven countries, the privatization of state industries was also an important reason for increased foreign investment. As was more or less to be expected, no country study has concluded that debt relief had any influence on this increase in foreign investment. Other factors were more important, e.g. macro-economic stability, liberalization of the foreign exchange market or higher economic growth. In Mozambique, however, where foreign investment increased spectacularly after 1999, agreements with the World Bank and the International Monetary Fund (IMF) and compliance with those agreements were of influence. This was due particularly to the fact that a number of major foreign

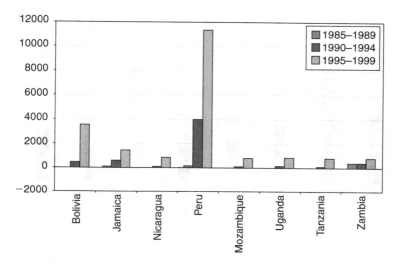

Figure 4.9 Net flows of foreign direct investment to the eight countries, 1985–1999, totals per period, in US$ millions (source: World Bank, Global Development Finance, 2002).

projects were financed partly (up to two-thirds) with official loans[8] or loans guaranteed by export credit agencies (ECAs). Without those loans, and thus without the seal of approval from the World Bank and the IMF, those foreign investment projects would not have come about.

Investment

In all eight countries except Tanzania, investment as per cent of GDP increased in the 1990s (Figure 4.10). Again, however, debt relief was relatively unimportant in most countries. Only in Peru was the elimination of arrears to the multilaterals of significance. This removed Peru from the international black list and had a psychological effect on investors. From 1993 onwards, investments began to increase, mostly in the construction sector, so that they had positive short-term effects on growth and employment but less effect in the long term. In the other countries, different factors were of more influence on the increase in investments, such as greater political and macro-economic stability, economic growth and increased foreign aid which enabled the construction sector to develop. The latter was particularly significant for Nicaragua in 1999, after hurricane Mitch had devastated the country in late 1998, but was also important in the other countries except Jamaica and Peru. In Mozambique, debt

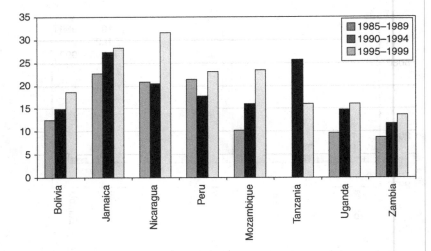

Figure 4.10 Investment (Gross fixed capital formation) in per cent of GDP in the eight countries, 1985–1999 (No data available for Tanzania before 1990), averages over three periods (source: Calculated on the basis of data from World Bank, World Development Indicators CD-ROM, 2001).

relief did not influence investment, but the conscientious debt payments to the multilaterals and the Paris Club seemed to have had a favourable effect as they enabled a flow of foreign aid from Paris Club members, which was considered essential for the stability and development of Mozambique.

In most countries, the level of investment in per cent of GDP is still not very high, with the exception of Jamaica and, more recently, Nicaragua. In Bolivia, Tanzania, Uganda and Zambia, investments were very low.[9] The majority of country studies attribute these low investments to such factors as high domestic interest rates, lack of good physical infrastructure, e.g. roads, harbours or telecommunication systems, or high cost of utilities such as water, electricity and telecommunications. Moreover, some countries still suffer considerable political unrest, while serious corruption is also an obstacle to investment. High levels of debt or debt overhang seem to play little, if any role for private investors.

Summary of the stock effect

Table 4.2 combines the quantitative results of the various indicators of creditworthiness with the more qualitative analysis of the influence of debt

Table 4.2 Summary of ultimate stock effects in the eight countries[a]

	Net total inflow of loans		Loans to private sector		Foreign Direct Investment		Portfolio flows		Investment	
	Result	DR	Result	DR	Result	DR	Result	DR	Result	DR
Bolivia	+	no	++	yes	++	no	n.a.		+	no
Jamaica	–		+[b]	yes	+	no	n.a.		+	no
Nicaragua	0		0		+	no	n.a.		+	no
Peru	+	yes	++	yes	+	no	+		+	yes
Mozambique	+	no	0		+	no	n.a.	yes	+	no
Tanzania	–		0		+	no	n.a.		+	no
Uganda	–		0				n.a.		–	
Zambia	–				+	no	n.a.		+	no

Source: Text and country studies

Notes

a The 'Result' columns show whether the variable has increased (+) or decreased (–), has remained unchanged (0) or is not applicable (n.a.) because the inflow does not exist. The column DR shows whether or not debt relief has contributed to a positive result.

b In Jamaica this concerns particularly *private loans to the government*, but loans to the private sector also increased somewhat.

relief (partly on the basis of the in-depth country studies). In Peru, debt relief had a clear stock effect, running via an effect on the inflow of loans, of loans to the private sector, portfolio equity flows and increased domestic investment. Bolivia and Jamaica also show a slight stock effect but only through the inflow of loans in general (Bolivia) or an inflow of loans to the private sector (Jamaica). In the other countries, debt relief had no stock effect. This seems clearly to be due to the continuing debt over-hang in those countries, both in the form of considerable arrears on out-standing debt and in the form of a low ratio between debt service paid and debt service due.

Flow effect in the eight countries

Debt relief is similar to aid insofar as it leads to an increased flow of funds. Such an increase can have positive effects on the balance of pay-ments through increased imports and on the government budget. As regards the latter, two positive effects are conceivable, namely a reduction of the deficit and an increase of expenditure. These immediate effects on the balance of payments and on the government budget are called here the intermediary flow effects and will be discussed first.

Greater public expenditure may give rise to two positive effects, i.e. increased public investment and increased social expenditure. The former can encourage private investment through 'crowding in', while increased social expenditure may lead to improvement of the social indicators. Public expenditure and its composition may be influenced by a possible flow effect of debt relief and, in addition, by policy conditions attached to that relief. This section therefore goes on to discuss possible effects on public investment and on social expenditure and social indicators.

Intermediary flow effects on the balance of payments and on the government budget

Insofar as there is an effect on the release of funds for the *balance of pay-ments*, there is no difference between debt relief and (other) foreign aid. Aid to Peru was minimal, and Jamaica received only limited quantities of aid during the first half of the 1990s. In the six low-income countries, aid had a greater effect than debt relief on the balance of payments, simply because the aid flow was far greater than the part of debt relief that freed resources. In Nicaragua, for example, such debt relief represented only 7 per cent of total aid in the 1990s. In these countries, aid thus led to more extra imports than did debt relief.[10] In Tanzania, actual debt service during the 1990s was only 19 per cent of foreign aid received in the same period.

This shows that debt payments and debt relief were of relatively little importance for these countries as compared to aid.

Debt relief and aid can also release funds for the government budget, but only non-project-tied aid, i.e. programme aid or macro-economic support, is comparable in this respect with debt relief. The larger portion of aid, however, was in the form of project aid. For example, in 1998, Africa as a whole received US$12 billion in foreign aid, but only US$3 billion was in the form of programme aid. This contrasted with US$9 billion paid in debt service. Thus, while highly indebted countries were given more aid (frequently also those with ineffective policies), that aid was only partially appropriate for debt payments. From the point of view of government budgets, therefore, the net flow was negative. The incoming flow of aid ensured that public *investment* could often be guaranteed, but outgoing debt payments supplanted *current expenditure*. Another problem was that both aid and debt payments fluctuated strongly and thus complicated the management of public finances (Sachs *et al.* 1999).

Chapter 3 concluded that only in Bolivia and Jamaica did debt relief help to reduce the outflow of debt payments and also stabilized debt service. In five countries, it had only a slight effect on debt service, and the effect was zero in Peru. In Jamaica and Bolivia, in particular, debt relief may have had positive effects on the government budget. In the years that it received debt relief, Jamaica's public deficit of 6 per cent of GDP in 1990 was gradually converted into a surplus of 4 per cent in 1994, while public expenditure as per cent of GDP remained constant. Bolivia also reduced its public deficit in the first half of the decade, while expenditure gradually rose throughout the 1990s, as did current expenditure.

In Nicaragua and the four African countries, debt relief had little influence on the outflow of debt payments, but public deficits did decrease at the start of the 1990s. At the same time, public expenditure as per cent of GDP fell in many years, for example, in reaction to a temporary reduction in programme aid (e.g. due to donors' dissatisfaction with the quality of governance) or due to increased debt payments.

In the six low-income countries investigated, public investment was mostly financed with foreign aid. Current expenditure for those investments (salaries, school books and maintenance) was paid by the country. While project aid was largely independent of donor opinions about 'good governance' and was thus more continuous, current expenditure suffered from setbacks in programme aid or from extra debt payments. In practice, current expenditure decreased in all six countries except Bolivia during the 1990s, thus making apparent the negative effects of the combination of considerable project aid, little debt relief and little freely disposable aid.

Public investment and 'crowding in'

As noted above, the volume of public investment in the six low-income countries depended above all on the amount of project aid received rather than on debt relief. In Jamaica, debt relief seems to have had no influence on public investment either: while total expenditure as per cent of GDP remained steady between 1990 and 1994, the share of capital expenditure fluctuated slightly but without showing any clear trend. If debt relief has no effect on public investment, there can also be no flow effect on private investment through 'crowding in'.

Social expenditure and social indicators

This section investigates the possible flow effect of debt relief, aid and policy conditions for debt relief on public expenditure in the social sectors, while possible consequences for the improvement of social indicators are also examined.

A first outcome is that during the 1990s many countries experienced a shift in the government's investment portfolio towards greater expenditure on the social sectors, e.g. for education and health care. This was due to three factors which to varying degrees played a role in the eight countries:

1   an autonomous trend: the privatization of state industries, as a result of which government invested less in production capacity and thus had more funds available for social investment (particularly Bolivia and Peru);

2   donor priorities: donors gradually directed their attention more towards social projects and away from infrastructure or production; almost all countries have set up a Social Investment Fund that invests in social infrastructure and that receives many foreign loans; project aid and, in Peru, the new loans are almost always tied to increasing capital expenditure, i.e. investments;

3   donor conditionality: in countries with a Multilateral Debt Fund (MDF) and later with a collective fund for general budget support, participating donors usually require that released funds be used to build up the social infrastructure. Exceptions in this respect include Tanzania, where the MDF and later the Poverty Reduction Budget Support (PRBS) group aim at protecting *current* expenditure in social sectors, and Uganda where the MDF and its follow-up the Poverty Action Fund (PAF) aim at increasing expenditure on the social sectors in general.

In five of the six heavily indebted poor countries (HIPCs) (Bolivia is the exception), however, *current* expenditure on the social sectors decreased in the 1990s. In some countries, even *total* public expenditure on the social sectors as per cent of GDP decreased during that decade. This applied, for example, to expenditure on health care in Mozambique, Uganda and Tanzania and on education in Mozambique, Tanzania and Zambia (World Bank 2002).[11] In Zambia, this was caused particularly by falling total public expenditure: in per cent of the latter, spending on the social sectors increased – in agreement with the requirements of Zambia's donors. Project aid and policy conditionality thus influenced greater investment in the social sectors, but the shortage of freely expendable aid together with high debt payments (too little debt relief) meant that current expenditure on the social sectors could not grow at the same rate or even decreased.

The question now is whether and in how far these sometimes increasing investments and decreasing current expenditure have influenced social indicators. With respect to a couple of crucial health indicators, for example, infant mortality has fallen in all countries except Zambia. Life expectancy rose in all countries except those plagued by HIV/AIDS: Tanzania, Uganda and Zambia (Table 4.3). Infant mortality reacts more quickly than life expectancy to changes in access to, and the quality of, health care provisions, while the latter is partly the result of long-term developments. However, the reduction of infant mortality is not always due to improved health care. In Bolivia, and probably also in other countries, increased access to clean water is a vital factor. The Social Investment Fund, active in Bolivia since 1986, has invested a great deal in the water sector. Improved hygiene and counselling through educational services can also have had a favourable influence on decreasing infant mortality.

Table 4.3 Selected health indicators for the eight countries, 1990 and 1997

	Infant mortality (per 1000)		*Life expectancy*	
	1990	*1997*	*1990*	*1997*
Bolivia	80	62	58	61
Jamaica	25	22	73	75
Nicaragua	51	37	64	68
Peru	54	36	66	69
Mozambique	150	135	43	45
Tanzania	115	99	50	48
Uganda	104	99	47	42
Zambia	107	113	49	43

Source: World Bank, World Development Indicators CD-ROM, 2002.

Table 4.4 Selected education indicators for the eight countries, 1990 and 1998 (or 1999)

	Pupil/teacher ratio, primary school		Primary school enrolment, gross (%)		Secondary school enrolment, gross (%)		Illiteracy (%)	
	1990	1998[a]	1990	1998[b]	1990	1998[b]	1990	1999
Bolivia	25	26	95	106	37	40	22	15
Jamaica	37	31	101	98	65	90	18	14
Nicaragua	33	36	94	102	40	50	37	34
Peru	29	25	118	126	67	81	14	11
Mozambique	55	61	67	71	8	9	67	57
Tanzania	35	38	70	65	5	7	37	26
Uganda	29	60	71	154	13	16	44	34
Zambia	44	45	99	86	24	27	32	23

Source: World Bank, World Development Indicators CD-ROM, 2002.

Notes
a For Bolivia and Nicaragua 1997.
b For Bolivia 1996; for Nicaragua and Tanzania 1997.

The fall in infant mortality is particularly noticeable in Bolivia, Nicaragua and Peru. In Jamaica, it had occurred much earlier. The rate is still very high in the four African countries, showing hardly any improvement. This may be due to decreasing (total) public expenditure on health care in three of the four countries. In 1989, Zambia introduced user fees for basic health care and basic education, which possibly had a negative effect on access to these services.

The reduction of current expenditure on education is reflected in a worsening of the pupil/teacher ratio in six of the eight countries (Table 4.4), signifying that the quality of education probably deteriorated. The greatest rise in the pupil/teacher ratio is to be seen in Uganda where, in 1997, the president proclaimed universal access to basic education (apparently without the facilities being available); in Mozambique, Tanzania, Nicaragua, Bolivia and Zambia, there is also evidence of deterioration in this indicator.

Primary school enrolment rates increased in six of the eight countries and most in Uganda. New school buildings erected by the Social Investment Funds probably had an effect (though apparently not in Zambia), as did the new policy in Uganda. In Tanzania and Zambia, however, primary school enrolment actually fell. Together with Mozambique, these are the countries where actual government education budgets fell in the 1990s. In Tanzania, it was not until 2000 that registration fees for basic education were abolished, influenced by extra funds made available under MDF/PRBS, and in 2001 also the tuition fees. Previously, the government had had no funds available for this purpose. Primary school enrolment will now possibly increase.

Secondary school enrolment rates increased in all countries, and illiteracy fell (Table 4.4), probably due to long-term trends rather than in response to policy in the 1990s. In the African countries, however, particularly in Tanzania and Mozambique, secondary school enrolment is still very low.

Long-term debt sustainability

Sustainability in relation to exports and income

According to Gillis *et al.* (1996: 414), an external debt can be sustainable for the balance of payments in the long term, even in combination with a trade deficit, if the growth rate of exports is higher than the average interest to be paid on the debt. In the long term, the debt then tends towards:

$$\frac{D}{X} = \frac{a}{g_x - i}$$

where D = debt, X = exports, a = trade deficit as per cent of exports, i.e. $(M - X)/X$, M = imports, g_x = growth rate of exports and i = average interest rate on debt.

A trade deficit in principle causes external debt to increase annually because it has to be financed with loans. Since many debtor countries are in a position to finance part of their trade deficit with Official Development Assistance (ODA) grants, this study investigates the 'adjusted trade deficit', calculated as follows: $(M - X - Grants)/X$. The expected value of the debt/export ratio (D/X), which comes about if all variables remain constant for a long time, can be calculated and compared to the critical value for a sustainable debt. According to the enhanced HIPC initiative, this critical value is currently 150 per cent.[12] If export growth is less than the interest rate on foreign debt, a trade *surplus* is needed to make the debt sustainable: $(M - X - Grants) < 0$.

Table 4.5 shows that in all eight countries except Zambia, export growth[13] was higher than the average interest on new loans: column 3 shows a positive figure, which is largest for Nicaragua, Mozambique, Uganda and Tanzania. The adjusted trade deficit is positive in all countries, i.e. imports exceed exports plus grants, giving rise to a deficit

Table 4.5 Calculation of long-term sustainability of the debt/export ratio, in per cent

	Interest[a] (1)	g_x^b (2)	$g_x - i$ (3)	Adjusted trade deficit[c] (4)	Debt/export[d] (4/3)
Bolivia	3.3	5.6	2.4	28.5	1214
Jamaica	6.9	7.4	0.5	4.2	850
Nicaragua	3.5	12.9	9.4	88.0	936
Peru	6.0	7.0	1.1	38.5	3630
Mozambique	1.2	8.9	7.8	29.4	378
Tanzania	1.3	8.6	7.2	61.5	852
Uganda	1.1	9.8	8.7	84.3	971
Zambia	2.0	-3.9	-5.9	15.9	

Sources: World Bank, Global Development Finance, 2002; and on grants: World Bank, World Development Indicators, 2002.

Notes
a Average over 1990–1999 of the average interest rate on new foreign loans, in per cent.
b Average annual growth rate of exports of goods and services, 1990–1999, in percentages.
c Average 1990–1999 of (imports less exports less grants)/exports, in per cent. Source: GDF 2002;
d Calculated 'long-term' debt/export ratio in percentages, i.e. the D/X ratio that exists if all variables remain the same. Any deviations in dividing column (4) by column (3) are due to calculations with unrounded figures in columns (3) and (4); the results are multiplied by 100 in order to express the quotient in per cent. If columns 3 or 4 show a negative figure, the D/X ratio cannot meaningfully be calculated.

(column 4). Although with the exception of Zambia, all countries can afford a trade deficit since export growth is greater than the interest rate, in the HIPCs Bolivia, Nicaragua, Mozambique, Uganda and Tanzania that deficit is far too large to allow debt to be sustainable in the longer run (column 5 = 4/3; but see note d to Table 4.5). As a result, even if the debt were brought down to a sustainable level, e.g. through the HIPC initiative, it will in time inevitably again become unsustainable if the trade deficit does not fall.[14]

At present, the adjusted trade deficits can be as large as they are, because these countries receive many loans. It can also be concluded that the large volume of loans *causes* the large trade deficits. For the HIPCs, those are chiefly loans from the IFIs. In theory, it is possible that these loans lead to higher exports in the future, with which payments of interest and amortization can be made. In practice, however, this has proven impossible and is even less feasible when most loans are destined to the social sectors, as is recently the case. For future sustainability, it is important that a larger part of the trade deficit be financed with grants and/or that the volume of external loans to these countries should decrease. Bolivia has the additional problem that the average interest rate is already much higher than in the other HIPCs. The country has borrowed from non-concessional multilateral sources such as the Andean Development Corporation. Future sustainability is therefore even more in danger than in the other HIPCs.

In the middle-income countries Peru and Jamaica, the margin between export growth and interest is very small. According to this analysis, long-term unsustainability is greatest in Peru which is not entitled to debt relief under the HIPC initiative. In practice, part of Peru's trade deficit (and also of Bolivia's) is financed with foreign direct investment over which interest need not be paid. Nevertheless, the Peruvian trade deficit also appears to be too large. Zambia should really have a trade surplus if its debt is to be sustainable. Because it does not, it is impossible to calculate the long-term debt/export ratio.

The long-term sustainability of the debt in relation to income, the debt/GDP ratio can be similarly examined. A debt can be sustainable for the economy in the long run, even in combination with a savings deficit, if the growth rate of GDP is higher than the average interest due. The debt then tends towards:

$$\frac{D}{Y} = \frac{v - s}{g_y - i}$$

where Y = GDP, $v = I/Y$, the investment ratio, $s = S/Y$, the savings ratio and g_y = growth rate of GDP.

The savings deficit $[v - s$ or $(I - S)/Y]$ causes external debt to increase each year, assuming that it is financed by loans. Part of it, however, is financed with foreign grants. Therefore, the savings deficit may be adjusted to read as follows: $(I - S - Grants)/Y$. The value of the long-term debt/GDP ratio can then be calculated and compared with the critical value, usually set at 60 per cent.[15]

In four of the eight countries, the average growth of GDP in the 1990s was lower than the interest on new loans (Table 4.6). These countries should really have an adjusted savings *surplus*, but that is only the case in Zambia. In Mozambique, the growth rate of GDP is far higher than the average interest, but that country has an adjusted savings surplus although it could afford a deficit. Mozambique's debt is thus sustainable in the long run if the trends of the 1990s in interest, investments, savings, aid and economic growth continue. It would in fact be better for long-term prospects if the country invested more, i.e. would have a savings deficit.

The three countries where growth is higher than the interest rate all have too high a savings deficit for a sustainable debt; yet Uganda is close to the critical value. Growth has been too low in Bolivia, and in Tanzania the savings deficit is too large. Nicaragua, which should actually have a savings surplus, has the greatest savings deficit of all eight countries – a situation which clearly does not lead to a sustainable debt situation.

Table 4.6 Calculation of the long-term sustainability of the debt/GDP ratio, in per cent

	Interest[a]	g(GDP)[b]	g(GDP)-i	Adjusted savings deficit[c]	Debt/GDP[d]
	(1)	(2)	(3)	(4)	(4/3)
Bolivia	3.3	4.0	0.7	2.4	325
Jamaica	6.9	1.4	−5.4	5.2	
Nicaragua	3.5	2.8	−0.6	13.3	
Peru	6.0	3.1	−2.9	2.2	
Mozambique	1.2	5.5	4.3	−1.7	
Tanzania	1.3	3.1	1.8	8.1	455
Uganda	1.1	6.8	5.7	4.1	73
Zambia	2.0	0.2	−1.7	−6.7	

Sources: World Bank, Global Development Finance, and World Development Indicators, 2002.

Notes
a See Note a, Table 4.5.
b Average annual growth rate of GDP over 1990–1999 (based on figures in constant US$), in per cent.
c Average over 1990–1999 of (fixed investments minus gross domestic savings minus grants)/GDP, in nominal US$, in per cent.
d Calculated long-term debt/GDP ratio, in per cent. See also Note d, Table 4.5.

The prospects for long-term debt sustainability are thus not favourable. All eight countries have too large a deficit on the trade balance, while in half of them economic growth has not been high enough to justify continual savings deficits. In that respect, only Mozambique, Tanzania, Uganda and Bolivia are on the right side of the divide; savings deficits in the latter two, however, are at present too high.

This signifies that, even if the eight countries should now have a sustainable debt, the burden will rapidly become unsustainable again if trade deficits remain as large as they are at present. Those sizeable deficits could rapidly lead to new unpayable debt. If all other factors remain equal, however, trade deficits (aid-adjusted) can only come about if sufficient loans are offered.

For the six HIPCs in particular, trade deficits could become smaller if the international community, i.e. the multilateral banks, should restrict its lending. Chapter 3 pointed out that there is evidence of moral hazard among IFIs as they do not bear the cost if debtor countries are unable to repay their loans. The analysis here shows that this moral hazard apparently has induced the IFIs to continue to lend, even when that was ill-advised from the viewpoint of long-term debt sustainability.[16]

It should be emphasized that this concerns not only the World Bank and the IMF but also the regional development banks, particularly the Inter-American Development Bank (IDB) which is active in Latin America. The IDB receives major contributions to the Fund for Special Operations from bilateral donors, enabling it to provide concessional loans to the poorest developing countries in Latin America (the so-called IDA-only countries), of which there are only five in the region: Bolivia, Guyana, Haiti, Honduras and Nicaragua. As a result, IDB has had to extend many loans to countries such as Bolivia and Nicaragua – loans that cannot be repaid without new aid from bilateral donors. In both these countries, the new annual inflow from the IDB is greater than that from the World Bank. In Nicaragua, it amounts to roughly US$100–140 million per annum, about one-fifth of annual exports. When asked about the chances that Nicaragua would ever repay those loans in view of the unstable growth of national income and exports, the IDB representative in the country replied: 'There should be growth.'

Sustainability in relation to the government

Similarly, the sustainability of public debt can be analysed by comparing the interest rate with the growth of tax revenue and by examining whether the size of a country's budget deficit ensures that debt is sustainable in the long term. International data banks, however, do not include data on tax collection and government expenditure for all countries. In Bolivia,

Nicaragua and Peru, the average annual growth of public revenue[17] was clearly more than the average interest due (tax revenues grew at 8.6, 10.1 and 14.7 per cent, respectively), but in Jamaica, it was a little less (6.6 per cent). On the basis of IMF data presented in the country studies, public revenue in Tanzania increased by an average of 6.1 per cent per year between 1991/1992 and 1998/1999; in Uganda, government income increased by 9 per cent between 1990 and 1999. Given the average interest on foreign debts of these countries (Table 4.6), these two countries are thus able to maintain public deficits. In Zambia, total government income fell by 3.4 per cent per annum during the 1990s, so a government surplus is necessary for a sustainable debt in relation to revenues.

However, debt sustainability from the public sector point of view does not only depend on foreign debts but also on domestic debts of the public sector. In investigating sustainability of the public debt, the magnitude of the domestic debt needs to be known and also its average interest rate, thus enabling a total average interest rate to be calculated. The domestic debt burden in almost all eight countries has increased during the 1990s, mainly for the following reasons:

1   Governments began financing their deficits by issuing bonds, a possibility which had previously not existed. This had started early in Jamaica and Peru, occurred since the end of the 1980s in Tanzania, and since the 1990s in Bolivia and Nicaragua.

2   Many governments have had to take over domestic banks for whom bankruptcy threatened, usually again issuing bonds for the purpose. This was the major reason for the enormous increase in Jamaica's domestic debt around 1995. In the 1990s, Zambia also had to take over a bankrupt bank, while Nicaragua took over four in 2000 and 2001. In the period 1999–2001, the governments of Uganda and Mozambique were also forced to save loss-making banks. In all countries, problems with domestic banks seem to have resulted from premature liberalization and privatization of the financial sector, i.e. before adequate systems of regulation and supervision had been designed and put into operation. The high domestic debts in all these countries were thus due at least partly to policy conditions laid down by the IFIs.

3   In Nicaragua, the largest component of domestic debt was formed by special bonds that were issued to compensate the former owners of nationalized industries or other properties if those properties could not be returned to them.

4   In Bolivia and Peru, bonds were issued on a small scale in order to buy out foreign creditors: foreign debt was thus transformed into domestic debt.

Jamaica's domestic debt increased from 30 per cent of GDP in 1990 to 91 per cent in 1999 when it even exceeded external debt. Jamaica's public sector debt was thus not sustainable, even if only its domestic part is considered. In Tanzania, during the 1990s, interest payments on domestic debt equalled about those on foreign debt. In such countries as Nicaragua, Mozambique, Uganda and Zambia, payments on domestic debt increase rapidly, an important factor being that interest on domestic debt in these HIPCs was far higher than the average interest rate on foreign debt. External debts mostly have a low, concessional, interest, while domestic (market-based) interest rates are often high.

According to the rules of the HIPC initiative, central banks in HIPCs may not convert domestic debts into non-concessional foreign debts, although this could be more favourable in view of the high domestic interest rates. This is all the more paradoxical in that a large part of 'domestic debt' is probably in foreign hands. Domestic banks (the most important government bond-holders), for example, frequently belong to foreign conglomerates or to people who have safely moved a large part of their capital abroad. In Nicaragua, the holders of ownership compensations are often ex-Nicaraguans who have long enjoyed US nationality.

The rapid increase in domestic debts has various negative consequences. First, debt servicing entails high costs for government budgets. Just as foreign debt seems to become sustainable through the HIPC initiative, many HIPCs have to spend increasing amounts on the payment of domestic creditors. This puts in doubt that the HIPC initiative actually releases funds for social expenditure and poverty reduction, as intended.

Second, public sector demand on the domestic capital market causes local interest rates to escalate and consequently reduces investment. This occurs both directly, with high interest rates putting off investors, and indirectly, because privatized domestic banks prefer to buy publicly guaranteed debt titles to investing in riskier (private) production activities.

The conditionality effect

The Paris Club donors and creditors required that countries had an agreement with the IMF before they considered debt relief. Chapter 3 concluded that most countries in our sample managed to meet IMF's macroeconomic objectives, though sometimes only with the help of the foreign aid that accompanied the agreement. Structural reforms were carried out primarily if the country had already planned to introduce them. If not, implementation was extremely slow if it occurred at all. In the terminology of this book, it was not very efficient to attach policy conditions to debt relief. But it can also be questioned whether the conditions attached to debt relief were the appropriate ones to further economic growth, so whether conditions were *effective*.

During the last 20 years, developing countries in general have adopted policies that broadly tallied with World Bank and IMF requirements in their adjustment programmes – albeit with large delays. As a result, foreign exchange markets have been liberalized, state industries have been privatized, tariffs on foreign trade have been lowered, banks have been privatized and the financial sector liberalized.[18]

It was anticipated that such neo-liberal reforms would attract investments and thus stimulate economic growth. Although some of them certainly had a positive effect,[19] the neo-liberal policy does not seem to have solved the problems private investors at present experience and which therefore interfere with growth. The most obvious example provided by the countries studied in this book is that the financial sector has often been privatized and liberalized prematurely. This occurred before the government budget had been straightened out and inflation had fallen and also before an effective system of regulation and supervision of the banking sector had been developed.[20] In almost all countries involved in this evaluation, governments have found it necessary to intervene expensively when private banks were threatened with bankruptcy due to irresponsible lending behaviour or downright fraud (see 'Sustainability in relation to the government'). Partly because of this, many governments still have to cope with large deficits which keep interest rates high and make it easy for banks to earn a great deal of money on government bonds. Little credit then remains available for the private sector. In almost all countries, it was found that private investments were hampered by lack of credit and high interest rates.

In most countries, investments were also hampered by the lack of good roads and public utilities, while the latter are also highly priced. Economies on the government budget over many years have often caused poor maintenance of the road network and the construction of too few new roads. On the instigation of the IMF and the World Bank, most countries have privatized their public utilities, though usually only after considerable delay. It is questionable, however, whether this will produce better quality and lower prices. In many countries, public monopolies have been replaced by private ones. Moreover, privatization often reduces access to these facilities for people and enterprises in remote locations and/or with few means to pay (increased) rates.

Another problem common to many countries is that of corruption, which donors are generally keen to tackle – at least, officially. They criticize government leaders, for example during meetings of Consultative Groups,[21] and try to persuade them to fight corruption and to punish those proven guilty. It might be asked, however, whether donors in some respects have not stimulated corruption.

In the first place, cuts in government budgets have often caused civil service salaries to be lowered substantially. Economies were often necessary, of course, but insufficient attention was given to the structurally negative consequences of the ways in which they were implemented. Second, due to their dissatisfaction with the quality of the government administration, donors have often created parallel structures for their projects. Much foreign aid bypasses the government budget (60 per cent or more is no exception), and almost all funds destined for project aid are deposited in accounts that are not managed by government institutions. The result is a lack of transparency which makes management of the funds difficult and facilitates their misuse. Third, at election time, donors are inclined to support the government in power, certainly in a country that appears to be doing well economically and where donors have established a good working relationship with that government. This occurs even when donors are simultaneously dissatisfied with corrupt practices of the incumbent administration. That support sometimes takes the form of approving new loans and grants just before the elections, enabling the government to win (extra) votes. It also happens, however, that criticism regarding serious corruption is expressed only in private in order not to discredit the incumbent government in the eyes of its own population (Mozambique, 2001–2002) or that a Poverty Reduction Strategy Paper (PRSP) is approved even if almost all donors consider it 'a seal of approval for a corrupt government' (Nicaragua, 2001).

In sum, the contents of conditions set by the IMF and other donors is not always effective in enhancing growth, and messages sent by donors are sometimes ambiguous.

Conclusions

Although debt relief has led to only a slight reduction in outstanding debt, in seven of the eight countries examined debt did become more sustainable during the 1990s. Zambia formed the only exception. In all eight, however, the debt/GNP ratio was still above 40 per cent in 1999, and it was far higher in Nicaragua, Mozambique and Zambia. The debt/export ratio in all eight countries except Jamaica exceeded 250 per cent; in the six low-income (HIPC) countries, it was much higher.

As regards liquidity, all countries except Jamaica were still in an unfavourable position in 1999. As per cent of exports, debt service increased in Nicaragua, Peru and Zambia. In the latter two, the ratio was above 40 per cent in 1999. Bolivia, too, spent a great deal of its export income on debt repayments: it was 29 per cent at the end of the decade. Debt service amounted to about 20 per cent in Mozambique and Uganda and 16 per cent in Tanzania and Nicaragua. The latter two countries, however, still had sizeable arrears, so their liquidity was very weak.

In Bolivia and Peru, debt relief helped to eliminate the debt overhang. At the end of the 1990s, these countries were free of arrears and able to meet all their obligations. Jamaica also paid most of its debt obligations, but it hardly had any debt overhang at the start of the decade. Nicaragua, Mozambique and Tanzania still paid only about 10 per cent of the amounts they owed and Uganda and Zambia slightly more. In these five countries, debt relief did not eliminate the debt overhang.

In Peru, Bolivia and Jamaica, debt relief has influenced the increase of investments and/or the inflow of new capital for the public and/or the private sectors. In the other five countries, debt relief had no stock effect on credit-worthiness or investment. Although foreign investments increased in all eight countries and, with the exception of Tanzania, also domestic investment as percentage of GDP, this was not due to debt relief.

In two countries (Bolivia and Jamaica), positive flow effects on the government budget occurred due to resources released by debt relief. Public investment in the low-income countries, however, proved to depend mainly on the quantity of project aid and not on debt relief. Policy conditions and considerable project aid have frequently enlarged the volume of investment in the social sectors. In five of the six HIPCs, however (Bolivia is the exception), current expenditure on the social sectors lagged behind, particularly because programme aid and debt relief together were not sufficient to finance the payment of debt obligations. Increasing social investments seem to have had an influence on enrolment in basic education (but not in Tanzania and Zambia). On the other hand, the decreasing availability of funds for current expenditure probably meant that the quality of education has suffered.

Prospects for long-term debt sustainability are not favourable. Even if debts become sustainable in relation to exports in the short term, thanks to the HIPC initiative, this situation will soon be reversed if trade deficits remain at their present high levels. The moral hazard for the IFIs has given rise to too great a volume of loans. To ensure a sustainable debt level in the future, it is necessary that a larger portion of the trade deficits be financed from grants and/or that the volume of loans to these countries should decrease, particularly those from the IFIs.

With respect to the sustainability of the debt for the *government*, an additional fact is that all countries are faced with a rapidly increasing domestic debt on which far higher interest must be paid. In the six HIPCs, this may endanger any positive flow and stock effects of the HIPC initiative.

The conditions set for debt relief, namely that the country should have an agreement with the IMF, were often not implemented, but to the extent that countries followed the IMF advice, it was not always appropriate.

5 The relevance of debt relief

This chapter examines the degree to which debt relief provided in the 1990s was relevant; in other words, whether it contributed to economic growth. First, developments in the gross domestic product (GDP) of the eight countries are discussed, and factors that were of influence on trends in the growth rate are briefly analysed. Unless otherwise indicated, this analysis is based on the various country reports. It also considers whether and to what degree debt relief has been of influence on economic growth through the flow and stock effects discussed in Chapters 3 and 4. Not surprisingly, the contribution of debt relief proves to have been limited.

Debt relief can only be of relevance, of course, if the debt or debt repayments hinder economic growth. Thus, this chapter also examines the empirical evidence on the relationship between debt and economic growth, particularly insofar as it influences the relevance of debt relief and of specific modalities. In order to explain the limited contribution of debt relief to economic growth, some further analysis is presented which shows that the nature of the debt problems has changed in the 1990s and that the uncertainty on debt payments probably was a significant factor in hampering the growth of highly indebted countries. In the last section of this chapter, the results of the country experiences and of the econometric study are brought together, leading to a conclusion on why debt relief was of limited relevance during the 1990s.

Debt relief and economic growth in the eight countries

The four Latin-American countries in the group experienced very different growth trends during the 1990s (Figure 5.1). Jamaica was fairly prosperous at the beginning of the decade, but its economy stagnated completely from 1996 onwards. In Nicaragua, the situation was reversed to some extent: the economy started to grow only in 1994, and this growth con-

82   *The relevance of debt relief*

tinued until the end of the decade, with a peak in 1999 due to the aid received after hurricane Mitch. Bolivia showed the most stable growth pattern throughout the period, but that seemed to come to an end in 1999. Peru's growth was the most volatile, with high peaks in the middle of the decade and low or negative growth prior to 1993 and again after 1998.

Bolivia conquered hyperinflation as long ago as 1986. Since then the country had benefited each year from a major inflow of new multilateral loans and bilateral grants. Debt relief helped to release funds, but in quantitative terms, aid and loans had a much greater influence on imports and government investments. Moreover, debt service remained high, partly due to the inflow of new loans. As shown in Chapters 3 and 4, debt relief had a minor flow effect and also a small stock effect. Private investment was still low in Bolivia, as was average growth throughout the decade, i.e. 3.9 per cent. The most important reasons for the decline in 1999 were the low prices for zinc, copper and tin and the hard line taken against coca growers, which caused loss of income as well as social unrest which in turn pulled the economy down. The years of economic growth have not led to the economy becoming less dependent on primary (and illegal) exports. Even after extensive privatizations, 50 per cent of employment in the formal sector is in the public sector.

Jamaica managed to bring inflation down in the first few years of the decade and also liberalized its economy, including the foreign exchange market and the financial sector. At first, this was accompanied by eco-

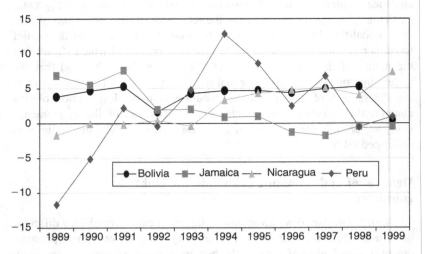

Figure 5.1 GDP growth in Bolivia, Jamaica, Nicaragua and Peru, 1989–1999, in per cent (source: World Bank, World Development Indicators CD-ROM, 2002).

nomic growth, but it also led to a credit boom and to irresponsible lending behaviour on the part of domestic financial conglomerates (Kirkpatrick and Tennant 2002). In 1995 and 1996, a number of those conglomerates threatened to go bankrupt due to inadequate regulation and supervision of the banking system. The government then intervened in the banks in order to protect small savers and to prevent capital flight. The public deficit rose substantially, causing interest rates to climb and the exchange rate to appreciate. Investments fell, as did exports, leading to negative economic growth after 1996.[1] Jamaica only enjoyed debt relief in the first half of the decade, which possibly had some positive influence on growth in that period (Chapters 3 and 4): the flow of debt payments decreased thanks to debt relief and the public deficit was turned around into a surplus. In addition, there was possibly some stock effect because the government gained access to private loans. External debt was reasonably sustainable at the start of the decade and the external debt situation has improved further, so that Jamaica was creditworthy in that respect. By 1999, however, the domestic debt was far greater than the external debt, and its burden was in itself unsustainable.

In 1991, *Nicaragua* managed to overcome hyperinflation, but economic growth came much later. Arrears with the International Financial Institutions (IFIs) were eliminated with the aid of bilateral loans and grants; however, this did not lead immediately to a net inflow of funds from those institutions because bridging loans first had to be repaid. In the first years of the decade, the political situation was still very unstable and investors adopted a 'wait-and-see' attitude. Around the mid-1990s, investments and exports started to increase as well as economic growth. The latter was based on the construction industry and on trade and later also on exports from tax-free zones (*maquila*). Although Nicaragua shows the greatest debt reduction of all eight countries, only 5 per cent of that actually freed resources for imports and government expenditure. This was due above all to the country's substantial arrears. These became smaller in the course of the decade, thanks to debt relief, but they were still considerable. By 1999, external debt was still staggeringly high and, in relation to gross national product (GNP), still the largest of all eight countries. In sum, debt relief only had a small flow effect and no stock effect on economic growth in this period.

In *Peru*, debt relief did not release resources at all because it was used entirely to eliminate arrears. This cleared the way for new loans from multilateral institutions (from 1991) and, after 1996, also for an inflow of private capital. While there was thus no flow effect in Peru, the stock effect was substantial: debt relief restored the country's creditworthiness and had a positive influence on investments, including foreign investment.

High growth after 1993 was also caused by the adoption of a successful stabilization policy, which suppressed inflation and initiated the recovery. The political tide began to turn around the middle of the decade and later also the economic situation. The Fujimori government was guilty of human rights abuses and of corruption yet retained the support of the international community. In 1996, a tighter budgetary and monetary policy led to a record inflow of foreign capital. When the Asia crisis broke out in 1997, however, that capital flowed just as rapidly out of the country, with major negative consequences for the economy. Peru now pays all its debt obligations and is thus creditworthy, but in 1999 used a high 40 per cent of its exports for the purpose. In the longer term, Peru's debt burden was shown not to be sustainable, particularly because of its large trade deficit.

In Africa, Uganda and Mozambique were the success stories in the 1990s, each with a very high growth rate, particularly since 1992 (Figure 5.2). They were also donor darlings. The Tanzanian economy revived at the end of the 1980s but stagnated early in the 1990s. Since 1995, growth has been reasonably high and stable. In Zambia, growth has fluctuated strongly from year to year, and this country with a stagnating economy throughout the 1990s was clearly the worst off of the four African nations investigated.

In *Mozambique*, the destructive civil war did not come to an end until 1992. The economy has grown solidly since 1993, partly due to a catch-up effect after the earlier decline: the end of the war enabled the return of refugees, who immediately started to grow crops. The country has

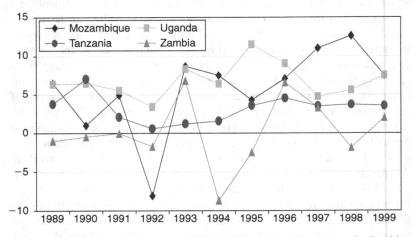

Figure 5.2 GDP growth in Mozambique, Tanzania, Uganda and Zambia, 1989–1999 in per cent (source: World Bank, World Development Indicators CD-ROM, 2002).

received a huge amount of foreign aid that had a positive effect on public investment and also furthered construction and trading activities. Debt relief provided by the Paris Club had some influence on the government's actual debt service payments in the second half of the decade because Mozambique then always paid Club members. The country is in arrears to other creditors, however, and although the debt stock fell slightly during the decade, those arrears have hardly been reduced. Moreover, in relation to exports, Mozambique still had the largest debt of all eight countries in 1999. Debt relief thus had only a limited flow effect and no stock effect on economic growth. Growth was mainly due to other factors.

Since 1987, *Uganda* has shown a fairly stable and high economic growth (approximately 6 per cent per annum), with a small slump in 1992 when it had a serious difference of opinion with the donors. Growth was initially due to stability after the end of the civil war and, in the 1990s, was based principally on the construction and manufacturing industries as well as on favourable terms of trade due to high coffee prices in the middle of the decade. Substantial aid also promoted growth, as did the liberalization of the foreign exchange market and of domestic trade. The high growth rate increased the confidence of investors, leading to the return of Asians with their capital and to other foreign investment. In all this, debt relief played hardly any role, particularly because the major part of Uganda's debt was multilateral. This meant relatively little debt relief during the 1990s, while the small amounts provided by the Paris Club had almost no flow effect owing to the great arrears. The debt itself has grown, but its sustainability has also increased thanks to the growth of GNP and exports. During the last few years of the decade, however, growth and also exports stagnated, due chiefly to falling coffee prices on the world market. Also in this country, the relevance of debt relief was very limited and growth was due to other factors.

Tanzania's debt was built up during the 1970s and 1980s when donors financed investments by state industries on a large scale with grants and with loans that were mostly non-concessional. When the development model supported by the donors proved ineffective, Tanzania was left with a massive debt and, at the start of the 1990s, also with towering arrears. Besides these, the small amount of debt relief pales into insignificance. Until the middle of the decade, Tanzania received mostly restructuring of a limited part of its debt service through Paris Club agreements. This had almost no effect on the flow of debt service paid. Only a small part of the debt was cancelled (more than in Jamaica and Peru but less than in all other countries), and arrears (as percentage of total outstanding debt) did not decrease at all throughout the decade. Debt has fallen in relation to GNP and exports, but that was due solely to the latter's growth. The fact that these indicators improved had no positive effect on investments or on the inflow of foreign private capital. In practice, investments fell. Against the background of sizeable new aid flows since 1986 when the country began to implement structural adjustment programmes, growth of the Tanzanian economy has been limited. During the 1990s, growth was based on construction, mining and tourism, the two latter of which started to attract foreign investment. The important agricultural sector lagged behind, however.

Of all eight countries, *Zambia* shows the most disappointing growth rate, averaging zero growth per annum during the 1990s, meaning that per capita growth was negative. After a split with the IFIs in the second half of the 1980s, the country started to implement an adjustment programme with IFI support in 1991. The sequence of the various measures was not always adequate, however. The financial sector and international financial flows were liberalized before inflation had been brought down and before adequate regulation and supervision of the banking system was introduced. Inflation remained high despite heavy cutbacks in the government budget, and this was partly due to capital flight. High inflation meant that tax revenue was disappointingly low; as a result, public deficits persisted, leading to continued inflation and high interest rates. Another problem was that the government withdrew hastily from the marketing of agricultural products. In Zambia, that meant an end to the subsidized growing of corn, while infrastructure and credit were insufficient to allow private trading in agricultural products to develop. The public deficit was also enlarged by the slow privatization of state industries, especially of the loss-making state copper mines. Economic growth was hampered further by the continuously low copper price on the world market. Debt relief contributed little to reducing the public deficit because it had hardly any effect on the flow of debt payments. On the contrary, those payments continued unrelentingly high throughout the decade, even increasing as per cent of exports. Although some debts were forgiven, debt stock and arrears both remained high in absolute terms. The stagnating economy and exports caused debt to increase in relation to GNP and exports.

These rough analyses show that debt relief had little effect on economic growth in all eight countries, with the possible exception of Peru which, however, still had a very high debt service in 1999. In general, other factors than debt relief seem to have had a greater effect on positive trends (if any) in growth rates. This manifestly slight relevance of debt relief is not surprising if the evaluation theory on which this book is based (Chapter 1) is taken into consideration. Chapters 3 and 4 have concluded that the efficiency and effectiveness of debt relief were not great. A major contribution to economic growth was thus not to be expected.

The question now is: What caused debt relief to be of such little relevance? In 1990, all eight countries clearly faced a debt position that was unsustainable (Chapter 2); consequently, it might have been expected that debt relief would contribute favourably to solving the problem.

Before digging deeper into the reasons for why debt relief was of little relevance, empirical literature on the relationship between debt and growth and the channels through which debt may affect growth is now examined. This sheds light on whether debt relief is relevant, and what modalities of debt relief, in particular, are likely to further economic growth.

Debt and growth

In principle, a country borrows in order to stimulate economic growth. Beyond a certain level, however, the debt can become too high and may then frustrate growth. In principle, a high debt level can prevent growth in two ways: through high debt payments or through a high debt stock. The first is known as the liquidity effect, the second as the debt overhang effect. In the first case, debt *payments* can have negative effects on the balance of payments and on public expenditure: as a result, the country can import less raw materials and machinery, and the government has less money available for physical and social infrastructure, for example. In the second case, the *high level of debt itself* discourages both investments and good policies because their yield will fall to the creditors rather than to the investors and the country's population.

If a country has a debt that compromises growth, debt relief may be relevant, i.e. may contribute to economic growth. But the modality of debt relief matters. If debt affects growth through the liquidity effect, a reduction in the net flow of debt payments through rescheduling payments obligations or through the provision of new loans or grants will be sufficient to secure economic growth again. If it is a case of debt overhang, however, debt forgiveness will be needed: the debt itself will have to be reduced and probably also the payment arrears.

Chapter 2 discussed how official creditors were long convinced that debtor countries principally suffered a liquidity problem. They tried to encourage those countries to pay their debts through a combination of relief on debt service (by restructuring and later also by partial forgiveness), grants and new loans – mainly concessional ones. The question is whether the diagnosis that debtors had to cope with liquidity problems was correct.

Empirical research into the relation between debt and economic growth uses standard growth equations and includes panel data for a large group of (low-income) countries and including several decades, usually averaging data for a three- or five-year period. These studies generally find a negative effect from debt on growth. Some studies just focus on the liquidity effect. Weeks (2000) finds a significant negative effect of debt service payments on growth in Latin America for the period 1970–1994. Hansen (2004) compares the effect of debt service payments with that of aid for 50 developing countries in the period 1974–1993. A reduction in debt service proved to have a significant but small effect on growth, while the effect of (an increase in) aid was much larger. He concludes that debt relief that is not additional to aid will have a limited effect.

Other studies include variables for the volume of both debt (in relation to exports or income) and debt service (in relation to exports or income). In this way, they attempt to distinguish between the debt overhang (stock) effect and the liquidity problem effect of a large debt (Cohen 1993; Elbadawi *et al.* 1997; Serieux and Samy 2001). Cohen found principally a liquidity effect; Elbadawi *et al.* found both a debt overhang effect and a liquidity effect; and Serieux and Samy also found both but mostly a negative effect on the import capacity of countries, so a liquidity effect.

More recent studies that include both the level of debt and a debt service variable in growth equations universally report that the debt stock variables have a significant effect on growth, while the debt service variable(s) do not (Pattillo *et al.* 2002, 2004; Clements *et al.* 2003; Cordella *et al.* 2005; Imbs and Ranciere 2005; Presbitero 2005).

Some studies explicitly search for non-linear relationships between growth and debt, so as to better approximate a possible debt overhang situation (Figure 1.2). Elbadawi *et al.* (1997) establish a debt overhang partly on the basis of the variable 'debt squared at time $t - 1$', which appears to have a negative effect on growth, while 'debt at time t' has a positive effect. Pattillo *et al.* (2002) find evidence for a non-linear relationship between debt and growth in the form of an inverted U. Similar results have been obtained by Clements *et al.* (2003), Pattillo *et al.* 2004 and Imbs and Ranciere (2005). This means that debt relief that reduces the debt stock is relevant for countries with debt levels above a certain threshold. On the other hand, Schclarek (2004) and Presbitero (2005) do not find evidence for a non-linear relationship. Finally, Cordella *et al.* (2005) do find a non-linear relationship but with two turning points: at a certain level, the debt begins to affect growth negatively, but at a very high level, it becomes irrelevant for growth. This would imply that small amounts of debt relief for countries above the highest threshold would not improve growth, but that larger amounts may do so. For heavily indebted poor countries (HIPCs) as a group, debt levels seem not to affect growth in this study. The same result, i.e. that debt levels do not affect growth, is also obtained for highly indebted countries and for countries with worse policies and institutions – categories that may overlap with the group of HIPCs but that are analytically more sound, as HIPCs have only been defined since 1999.

In sum, given the almost universally found negative relationship between debt and growth, debt relief should in principle be relevant. The more recent studies with more sophisticated econometric methods seem to show that it is not so much debt service that affects growth, but debt stocks, and especially above a certain threshold. This means that debt relief should be given in the form of forgiveness on stocks. However, the Cordella *et al.* study shows that small amounts of debt relief may not do the trick, because at very high debt levels, debt becomes irrelevant for growth. A positive growth effect on the heavily indebted countries can only be expected if debt stocks are reduced substantially. This gives two possible – not mutually excluding – explanations for the limited relevance of debt relief in the 1990s: the amounts were too small and debt relief was provided in the wrong modalities – too much rescheduling and forgiveness of flows and too little forgiveness on debt stocks.

However, there are a few problems with drawing specific conclusions for the relevance of debt relief in the 1990s and for specific modalities of debt relief from these econometric studies. First, the indicator for 'debt overhang' in these studies is simply the size of the debt.[2] However, the crucial aspect of a debt overhang is not the size as such, but the expected debt payments in relation to the size of the debt (Chapter 1). The relation between expected debt payments and size of debt depend on the extent of concessionality, but also on whether countries are paying those debts. The stock of unpaid arrears was large since the late 1980s (Figures 4.6 and 4.7). It is therefore not sufficient to use the net present value (NPV) of debt, as some studies do. To the contrary, more concessional debt relative to non-concessional debt may mean more, not less expected payments, due to the preferential creditor status of the IFIs providing the concessional loans. In order to take expected payments into account, another indicator is necessary.

Second, the nature of the debt problems may have changed in the 1990s as opposed to the 1970s and 1980s. As shown in Chapter 2, during the 1980s, the debt was mainly a Latin-American problem, and these countries had to increase their exports and reduce imports in order to release funds for debt service. The region experienced a large negative net transfer (Figure 3.1). It is not surprising that older studies find growth to be affected by a lack of liquidity and, in particular, a lack of import growth (Cohen 1993; Weeks 2000; Serieux and Samy 2001). In the 1990s, on the other hand, the then heavily indebted countries had access to new loans and grants, so there was much less need to curtail imports. The net transfer for sub-Saharan African countries always remained positive. Nevertheless,

Chapter 3 showed that debt service made heavy demands on government budgets because new loans and grants were primarily intended for projects, while governments had to settle debt payments out of their own revenue, or from uncertain macro-economic support. Debt payments can thus certainly have had a negative (liquidity) effect on economic growth during the 1990s – not through a reduced import capacity but through their demands on the state budget.

It is quite possible, however, that there was also a debt overhang effect in the 1990s. Many highly indebted countries did not pay all their obligations: some were rescheduled or forgiven, others were simply not paid. The classic debt overhang situation then probably prevails, in which debt payments may increase in the future, even if the debt itself decreases or remains the same, owing to improved payment capability. During the decade, these arrears sometimes diminished, but this often meant that relative to the total debt or to total debt service due, a higher debt service had to be paid. This brought about uncertainty about future debt payments. This uncertainty over future debt payments may be the essential aspect of debt overhang, and it is not adequately captured by taking the size of the debt as indicator.

Sachs *et al.* (1999) have shown that one of the problems with which highly indebted countries had to cope in the 1990s was that actual debt payments fluctuated strongly from year to year and that this also held for foreign aid. As a result, the efficient management of public finances became more difficult. Various authors have pointed out that debt payments, and also new loans or grants with which to meet payment obligations, depended partly on negotiations between debtor and creditors and that the outcome of such negotiations was uncertain for the debtor (Deshpande 1997; Sachs *et al.* 1999; UNCTAD 2000). Aid volatility has already been shown to hamper growth (Lensink and Morrissey 2000).

The fact that uncertainty regarding future payments can have a negative influence on investment has been shown with regard to Mexico (Claessens *et al.* 1994). It was not so much the reduced volume of debt payments that caused investment to increase after the Brady agreement but rather the reduced *fluctuations* in the level of debt payments. This shows that the negative effect of a debt overhang can be captured by looking at the volatility of debt payments.

Debt overhang in a new shape

The above-mentioned econometric studies into the relationship between debt and growth do not adequately capture the uncertainty of future payments as central aspect of debt overhang. Moreover, none of these studies has investigated whether the 1990s differed from earlier periods. In order to fill these gaps and in search of explanations for the results obtained so far, some original econometric research has been carried out in the context of this study (Dijkstra and Hermes 2003). The 1990s have been investigated separately, and an analysis has been made of whether the volatility of debt payments in that period had a negative influence on economic growth. If that is the case, it could help to explain the results found for the eight countries. Debt relief may have been of little relevance because the modalities in which it was provided did not reduce the volatility of debt payments.

As a first step, the relationship between debt and economic growth has been examined on the basis of analysis of 102 low- and middle-income countries for which data were available on GDP and growth-related variables as well as on debt variables. The period examined was that from 1970 up to and including 1998, and the data used are averages taken over three periods: the 1970s, the 1980s and the 1990s.

In an estimate of a standard growth equation covering the entire period, both the debt/GDP variable and the debt service/GDP had a significant negative effect on per capita growth, also when they were both included in the regression. However, when instead of ordinary least squares (OLS) with fixed effects per country a Generalized Method of Moments (GMM) method is applied, the results are slightly different.[3] The debt still has an important negative effect on economic growth, but the effect of debt payments on growth is no longer significant. So far, the results are fully in line with those of the other recent econometric studies mentioned above.[4]

Next, the results were analysed for each period separately. Unfortunately, only the OLS method could be used here because it was not possible to use the GMM for the separate periods[5] or to instrument the exogenous variables in any other way. The results must therefore be interpreted with appropriate caution. Nevertheless, some striking differences appear between the decades. In the 1970s and 1980s, a high debt has a significant negative effect on economic growth, but this disappears in the 1990s. It makes no difference whether or not debt service payments are included in the equation. Debt service payments are significant in all three periods, but if the debt is included in the equation, this significance only holds for the 1990s. This result appears to be in line with the irrelevance of the size of the debt found by Cordella *et al.* (2005) for countries at a high level of debt: for the group of HIPCs and for the most heavily indebted countries. It also confirms the hypothesis that debt service payments were a relevant factor in all three periods but that its effect was overstemmed by that of the debt size in the 1970s and 1980s – probably because there was still a close relationship between debt size and debt payments. In the 1990s, however, debt service payments affected growth negatively – despite a positive net resource flow.

In order to examine the effect of the uncertainty of debt payments, the volatility of debt payments is analysed, measured as the coefficient of variation[6] of the debt service/GDP ratio. Volatility appears to have been highest during the 1970s; in the 1980s, it was also higher than in the 1990s (Table 5.1). Since these figures are ten-year averages, however, a high volatility of debt payments can, ceteris paribus, be the consequence of a rapid change in the debt itself. Generally speaking, an annually increasing debt will be accompanied by an annually increasing debt service. Over a ten-year period, this gives a high coefficient of variation, but it is no evidence of fluctuations or uncertainty. It is thus important to include the change in the debt in the analysis. This was measured as the percentage change in the debt/GDP ratio over the ten-year period.

Tables 5.2–5.5 show the correlations between debt, debt payments, volatility in debt payments and changes in the debt stock, both for the whole period and per decade. Over the period as a whole, there is a fairly strong correlation between debt and debt payments (0.45) and also between change in the debt stock and the volatility of debt payments (0.50). Other correlations are far weaker (Table 5.2).

But it is much more interesting to look at these relationships for each period separately. The correlation coefficient between debt and debt payments is highest during the 1970s (0.71) and somewhat weaker in the 1980s and 1990s. This may be because debtors still paid practically all their obligations in the 1970s, but also because in the 1980s and 1990s, a greater part of loans has become concessional. The volatility of debt payments appears to be linked strongly to an increase in the debt stock in the 1970s and 1980s (0.55 in both periods), but the correlation was zero in the 1990s. This strong result shows that indeed, there has been a significant change in the nature of the debt problem in the 1990s. The volatility of debt payments in the 1990s (Table 5.1) can therefore not be attributed to a steady increase (or decrease) of debt in that period but is due to fluctuations in the debt or in debt payments. These fluctuations may thus be due to uncertainty regarding debt payments.

There seems to be little correlation between the size of debt payments and their volatility; insofar as such a correlation does exist (particularly in the 1980s), it is negative: the higher the payments, the less the volatility and vice versa. The linkage between the size of debt and the volatility of payments, on the other hand, is interesting: in the 1970s and 1980s, there was little correlation (in the 1970s, it was even negative), but in the 1990s, the correlation was reasonably strong (0.42). This seems to indicate that a high average debt in the latter period was coupled with considerable fluctuations in debt payments.

Table 5.1 Volatility of the debt payments/GDP ratio

	1970–1998	1970–1979	1980–1989	1990–1998	1970–1998[a]	1970–1979[a]	1980–1989[a]	1990–1998
Maximum	3.16	3.16	2.39	1.19	1.23	1.23	1.03	1.19
Minimum	0.03	0.03	0.11	0.05	0.03	0.03	0.11	0.05
Median	0.35	0.38	0.38	0.26	0.34	0.38	0.37	0.26
Mean	0.42	0.55	0.41	0.34	0.39	0.46	0.39	0.34
Standard deviation	0.34	0.48	0.28	0.22	0.23	0.26	0.19	0.22

Note
a Excluding four extreme outliers for the 1970s and one for the 1980s.

Table 5.2 Correlation matrix of debt variables, entire period (1970–1998)

	Debt[a]	Change in debt[b]	Debt payments[c]	Volatility[d]
Debt	1.00	0.01	0.45	−0.02
Change in debt		1.00	−0.23	0.50
Debt payments			1.00	−0.19
Volatility				1.00

Notes
a This is debt/GDP.
b This is the percentage change in the debt/GDP ratio over ten years.
c Debt payments/GDP.
d Coefficient of variation of (Debt payments/GDP) over ten years.

Table 5.3 Correlation matrix of debt variables, 1970s

	Debt	Change in debt	Debt payments	Volatility
Debt	1.00	−0.23	0.71	−0.21
Change in debt		1.00	−0.26	0.55
Debt payments			1.00	−0.18
Volatility				1.00

Table 5.4 Correlation matrix of debt variables, 1980s

	Debt	Change in debt	Debt payments	Volatility
Debt	1.00	0.33	0.43	0.05
Change in debt		1.00	−0.10	0.55
Debt payments			1.00	−0.36
Volatility				1.00

Table 5.5 Correlation matrix of debt variables, 1990s

	Debt	Change in debt	Debt payments	Volatility
Debt	1.00	−0.17	0.45	0.42
Change in debt		1.00	−0.37	0.00
Debt payments			1.00	−0.09
Volatility				1.00

The next step was to estimate the growth regression for each period, including the measure of volatility. In order to control for volatility resulting from a steady increase or decrease of debt stock, the change in the debt stock was also included. It was expected that this change in the debt stock had a negative effect on economic growth. In the 1970s and 1980s, the volatility of debt payments would probably not in itself have a significant negative effect on growth because volatility in those years proved strongly linked to the steady increase of the debt (see Tables 5.3 and 5.4). During the 1990s, that volatility could be expected to have a negative effect, apart from any negative effect caused by a change in the debt stock.

The GMM for the entire period shows that only the debt itself has a significant negative effect on growth, as before. There is no effect of the volatily if the whole period 1970–1998 is analysed. In the OLS regression, both debt and the change in debt are significant. Debt payments are only significant at the 10 per cent level, while the volatility of debt payments is not significant at all for the entire period. During the 1980s, among debt-related variables, debt itself and the changes in debt are significant, while in the 1970s, only the debt is significant.

The picture changes completely in the 1990s. As before, the debt itself is no longer significant, but debt payments are. At the same time, the change in debt and the volatility of debt payments are both significant, showing the expected minus sign. This may indicate that uncertainty about expected debt payments plays a role.

Altogether, the results can be seen as an indication that, during the 1990s, high debt had a negative effect on economic growth through high debt payments but also through the volatility of those payments. There may have been a case of debt overhang, expressed not so much in a high debt/GDP ratio but in the form of uncertainty regarding future debt payments.

Conclusion

In the first chapter, two contradictory opinions were presented on the relevance of debt relief: one group of authors argued that debt relief had been too little (Sachs 2002, 2005; Berlage *et al.* 2003; Hertz 2004), another group that there had already been too much debt relief and that it had been given to the wrong countries (Easterly 2002; Neumayer 2002). The empirical analysis presented in Chapters 3 and 4 has shown that actual debt relief provided during the 1990s proved to have limited relevance for economic growth. Flow, stock and conditionality effects were limited. It thus appears that the first group of authors is right in stating that debt relief has been insufficient but that there are many more explanations for the continuing debt problems. The second group of authors is right in pointing at problems in the conditionality mechanism for debt relief but not in their conclusion that there already has been too much debt relief.

From the analysis presented in this book, four factors can be distilled for explaining the limited relevance of debt relief in the 1990s:

1   Debt relief has been too limited.
2   Debt relief has been given in the inappropriate modalities.
3   There have been too many new loans, especially from the IFIs.
4   The conditionality mechanism for debt relief was not always beneficial and had several negative consequences.

These factors will now be discussed in more detail.

A first explanation for the limited relevance of debt relief during the 1990s is that it has been too little. This conclusion is in line with the econometric results of Cordella *et al.* (2005) and is also confirmed in this book. Although nominal debt relief has been large during the 1990s and has made a large dent in aid budgets (for example, it has taken €1.5 billion from the total 1990s aid budget of the Netherlands), the efficiency or immediate effects on the country studies have been small. Debt stocks have hardly been reduced, and debt relief did little to reduce actual flows of debt service, chiefly because many countries only paid a small part of their debt service due (Chapter 3). Flow effects could only be established for Jamaica and to a lesser extent Bolivia, and only in Peru, a substantial stock effect was observed.

A second explanation for these limited stock and flow effects is that debt was given in the wrong modalities. This was possibly the result of an inadequate diagnosis of the debt problem at around 1990 (Daseking and Powell 1999). Official creditors continued to think that debtor countries only had a liquidity problem and not a solvency problem. For this reason, they gave a large part of debt relief in the form of rescheduling as opposed to forgiveness and on flows as opposed to stocks. In addition, countries were provided with new loans and grants.

The conclusion that the applied debt relief modalities were not appropriate for the debt problems at hand is also confirmed in this book. The overwhelming majority of debt relief given during the 1990s was on debt service flows and not on stocks (Table 2.4). In our sample of eight countries, only Jamaica proved to have mainly a liquidity problem. For this country, the modality of rescheduling of debt service flows has worked. All other countries did not just have a liquidity problem but also a solvency problem. Only in Peru, this solvency problem was dealt with adequately, i.e. by removing (forgiving) *all* arrears – part of this successful dealing with the solvency problem can be ascribed to private creditors. The six low-income countries in the sample were mainly indebted to official creditors. The solvency problem of these countries was not addressed: they hardly received any stock relief, forgiveness on this flow relief was small and the flow relief did not even have a flow effect (in the sense of reducing actual debt service burdens) because it was mainly reducing debt service arrears. Due to the fact that not sufficient stock relief was given, arrears continued to be high and the debt overhang was not removed; uncertainty about future debt payments remained. Not surprisingly, all of these countries became eligible for the HIPC initiative in 1999.

The fact that debtor countries received so many new loans and grants is a third explanation for the limited relevance of debt relief. In all countries except Nicaragua, the average annual flow of new loan disbursements exceeded the annual average reductions in the debt stock as a result of debt relief (Tables 3.1 and 3.2). In itself, the large new inflows helped to perpetuate the debt problems: the debt service burden hardly diminished, and debt/export and debt/GDP ratios were still very high by the end of the decade. Only in one country, namely Peru, the new inflows can be seen as a positive stock effect of the earlier debt relief efforts. The country became creditworthy and regained access to private capital flows. Nevertheless, the debt/export and debt/GDP ratios in all eight countries proved to be unsustainable in the medium term if the trends of the 1990s with respect to trade deficit, export growth, income growth and average interest rates would continue.

One could argue that the combination of some flow relief with the provision of new aid and grants was a rational response to a wrong problem diagnosis. But the preceding chapters have shown that there were strong interests on the part of the creditors to maintain the flow of new loans. The overwhelming majority of new loans, especially to the six countries that became eligible for the enhanced HIPC initiative in 1999, was provided by multilateral development banks (Figure 3.6). These multilateral institutions were preferred creditors, so were always the first to be paid. This means they did not suffer the consequences of their irresponsible lending; in other words, they experienced moral hazard. The bilateral donors and creditors were in fact paying for this irresponsible lending: first by making these concessional loans from the IFIs to the low-income countries possible; second because the priority payment of multilateral debts reduced the value of bilateral claims, so requiring higher forgiveness; and third by providing new programme aid with which the debt service to the multilateral institutions could be paid. The moral hazard in the IFIs comes on top of other factors related to their own interests that drive a high loan volume of multilateral banks, as shown by other authors (Vaubel 1996; Dreher 2004; Ratha 2005).

The conditionality for debt relief is the fourth factor explaining the limited relevance of debt relief. Private creditors, and bilateral creditors not belonging to the Paris Club, did not attach conditions to their debt write-offs. The Paris Club, however, insisted that a country must first enter into an agreement with the International Monetary Fund (IMF) regarding structural adjustment. Most Paris Club countries were also donors. An IMF agreement was therefore a condition for both debt relief and for new aid loans and grants. Given the very high debt service burden in all debtor countries, they were under strong pressure to reach such agreement. Compliance with an IMF agreement was much less necessary, because bilateral creditors and donors committed a certain amount of flow relief for the period of the IMF agreement (usually three years). The IMF, for its part, had a strong interest in an agreement with the highly indebted countries because of the new inflow of programme aid that such an agreement would bring about and that could be used for paying earlier loans to the multilateral institutions. This institutional mechanism for the granting of debt relief and aid had several negative consequences.

First, it added to the uncertainty for the debtor country. Governments did not know when a new agreement with the IMF would be concluded or when they would reach an agreement with the Paris Club and – subsequently – with the individual Paris Club members. Moreover, they did not know how much debt relief they would ultimately receive and in what modalities or how much aid and new loans would become available. Most countries experienced large annual fluctuations in debt service paid and in aid. The empirical analysis presented in this chapter provides some evidence that debt service payments were indeed volatile in the 1990s and that this volatility had a negative impact on economic growth.

Second, as also concluded in many other studies, conditionality was not very effective in the sense that conditions were not always implemented. Countries only implement what they already intended to implement. Third, the conditionality that was meant to improve policies, in practice brought about adverse selection. Highly indebted poor countries not only received more new grants and loans than other poor countries, but there is also evidence that countries with worse policies (according to criteria as usually defined by the IFIs themselves) received more aid (Birdsall *et al.* 2003; Cordella *et al.* 2005). The large inflow of new loans from the IFIs, caused by moral hazard and self-interest, and the adverse selection that accompanied it, simultaneously perpetuated debt problems *and* bad policies.

Fourth, to the extent that conditions were implemented, they were not always appropriate for promoting economic growth. As discussed in Chapter 4, most developing countries that were dependent on aid and thus on good relationships with the IFIs did liberalize their economies during the past decades – although with large delays. These liberalizations and privatizations sometimes had negative consequences for growth and development. For example, financial sectors were often liberalized prematurely leading to high costs for the state budget when ailing banks had to be rescued. In general, it is increasingly recognized that rigidly liberalizing domestic economies is not giving the best development outcomes (Stiglitz 2002; White and Dijkstra 2003)[7] and that in general adjustment costs should be addressed when liberalization measures are carried out (Bhagwati 2004). In sum, the conditionality attached to debt relief contributed to the limited relevance of debt relief for economic growth and sometimes even had damaging effects.

6 The impact of debt relief since 2000 and prospects for the future

The aim of this chapter is to examine the impact of debt relief provided since 2000 and to assess the prospects for sustainable debt in the future. In order to answer the question whether debt relief in the new millennium has been relevant for economic growth, or at least more relevant than in the 1990s, it is important to consider the factors that hampered this relevance in the 1990s: limited amounts and inappropriate modalities, too many new loans and the influence of conditionality.

The main difference between the current decade and the 1990s is the implementation of the enhanced initiative for the heavily indebted poor countries (HIPCs) since 1999. The analysis of the impact of the HIPC initiative focuses on the years 2000–2005 (where possible, including 2006) and is based on a literature survey and on more in-depth analysis of the six HIPCs analysed in the preceding chapters. This chapter examines the consequence of the HIPC initiative for amounts and modalities of debt relief, of new loans and of changes in conditionality. In a final section of this chapter, possible effects of more recent debt initiatives will be assessed, such as the new Debt Sustainability Framework (DSF) and the Multilateral Debt Relief Initiative (MDRI). Since they only began to be implemented in 2005 and 2006, respectively, only the immediate effects and possible effects for the future can be dealt with.

The HIPC initiative: amounts and modalities

The HIPC initiative aims at reducing the net present value (NPV) of external debt to 150 per cent of exports. In order to compute the amount of debt relief needed, the average value of exports over the three years preceding the decision point is used. In principle, all creditors co-operate in this exercise. Contributions by the various groups of creditors to the total debt reduction are proportional, i.e. all groups reduce the NPV of their debt by the same percentage. The Paris Club does this by reducing the still outstanding debt stock (prior to the 'cut-off date'[1]) by up to 90 per cent in NPV terms, and more if needed. Multilateral institutions do so by annually forgiving a fixed percentage of the debt service on debt outstanding at decision point, over a 15- to 20-year period. Other bilateral creditors (not belonging to the Paris Club) and commercial creditors are encouraged to reduce the NPV of their debts by the same percentage.

The amount of debt relief under the enhanced HIPC initiative is greater than has ever previously been given. The international community thus recognized that debt relief had been insufficient during previous decades. For those countries qualifying for the initiative and meeting the conditions (see 'Conditionality' below), debt burdens have been reduced substantially. Another positive factor is that debts to *all* creditors are involved in the agreement, in other words, including those to International Financial Institutions (IFIs). In this way, the international community acknowledged that the multilateral debt burden formed part of the problem. Finally, the HIPC initiative implies a break with the past in focusing on forgiveness rather than rescheduling and on stock relief rather than flow relief. Once countries reach the completion point of the initiative, they know by how much their debt stocks will be reduced so that in principle, and to the extent that all creditors co-operate in the initiative, uncertainty on future debt payments is reduced.

The six low-income countries in the group of eight heavily indebted countries analysed in this book all qualified for the HIPC initiative. They reached the decision point of the initiative in 2000. By 2005, they had all reached the completion point as well (Table 2.3). They received substantial amounts of debt relief in the six years from 2000 onwards, while the non-HIPCs Jamaica and Peru hardly received any in this period (Table 6.1). Within the HIPC group, Bolivia and Uganda received the smallest amounts, but this can be at least partly explained from the fact that they had already obtained relief on the basis of HIPC 1. Furthermore, Uganda hardly had Paris Club debts to begin with. The share of forgiveness as opposed to rescheduling has increased in all countries as compared to the 1990s and fluctuates between 71 per cent for Uganda and 100 per cent for Bolivia (Figure 6.1). The share of stock relief as opposed to flow relief has also increased in all countries except Nicaragua (Figure 6.2).[2]

Comparing the annual amounts of forgiveness with the public debt stocks of the preceding year, it is clear that debt relief had more substantial effects on debt stocks in recent years (see first two bars per country in Figure 6.3). In all countries except Uganda, annual forgiveness in recent years is higher than in the 1990s and amounts to 5.6 per cent per year or more. In four out of six countries, the relative share of forgiveness is now also higher than the share of new loan disbursements (compare second and

Table 6.1 Debt relief for the eight countries, 1991–1999 and 2000–2005

	Total in US$ millions		Share forgiveness, in %		Share stock relief, in %	
	1991–1999	2000–2005	1991–1999	2000–2005	1991–1999	2000–2005
Bolivia	3489	1481	43	100	27	76
Jamaica	1595	25	34	100	28	0
Nicaragua	11065	3913	65	83	55	35
Peru	22345	172	11	88	37	0
Mozambique	4742	2972	56	91	31	85
Tanzania	2605	2388	53	84	0	29
Uganda	1394	731	65	71	31	53
Zambia	3812	2204	40	86	14	65

Source: World Bank, Global Development Finance online, 2006.

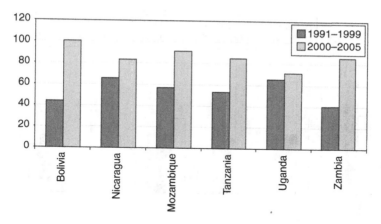

Figure 6.1 Average share of forgiveness in total debt relief to six HIPCs, 1991–1999 and 2000–2005, in per cent (source: World Bank, Global Development Finance online, 2007).

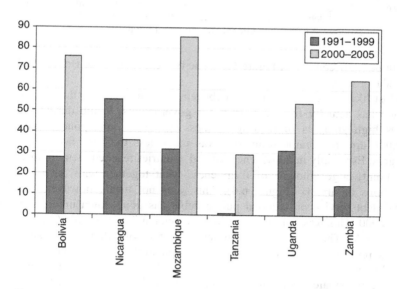

Figure 6.2 Share of stock relief in total debt relief to six HIPCs, 1991–1999 and 2000–2005, in per cent (source: World Bank, Global Development Finance, online, 2007).

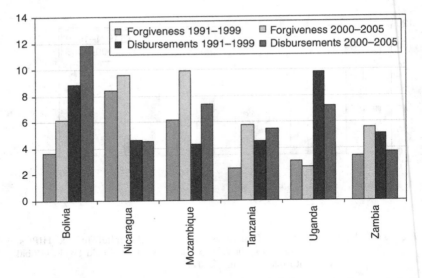

Figure 6.3 Average annual share of forgiveness and disbursements in per cent of
public debt stocks of preceding years, 1991–1999 and 2000–2005
(source: World Bank, Global Development Finance online, 2007).

fourth bars per country in Figure 6.3). The two exceptions are Bolivia and
Uganda.

Most likely, the greater part of debt relief provided during the present
decade has actually freed resources for governments. While during the
1990s high amounts of debt forgiveness generally corresponded with
negative arrears accumulation, this was much less the case from 2000
onwards. Especially in 2001, when several countries reached their completion point, large amounts of forgiveness went together with only tiny
reductions of arrears (Figure 6.4). This does not mean, however, that
actual debt service on external public debts has gone down universally
since 2000. This was only the case in Nicaragua and in Tanzania (Figures
6.5 and 6.6). The limited effect on actual debt service flows is probably
also the result of abundant new loans – the topic of the next section.

Debt sustainability has improved between 1999 and 2004 in all countries except Jamaica, while no data are available for Zambia (Figure 6.7).
Among the HIPCs, the largest fall in the debt-to-export ratio is registered
by Mozambique, and the smallest one in Uganda. In fact, the debt-to-
export ratio was still high in that country in 2004: 300 per cent. We do not
have access to figures on the NPV of the debts, which are lower than the
nominal values, but it can be expected that at least for Uganda, the 2004

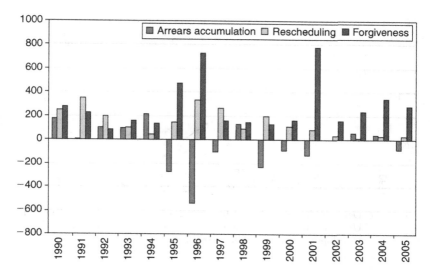

Figure 6.4 Averages for the six HIPCs of arrears accumulation, rescheduling and forgiveness, 1990–2005 (source: World Bank, Global Development Finance online, 2007).

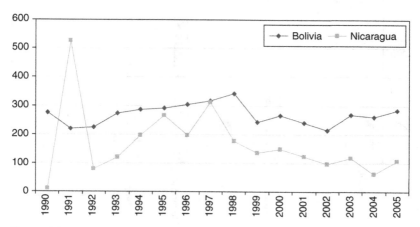

Figure 6.5 Debt service on public debt 1990–2005, Bolivia and Nicaragua, in millions of US$ (source: World Bank, Global Development Finance online, 2007).

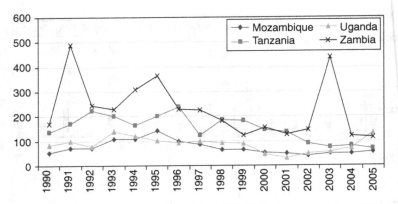

Figure 6.6 Debt service on public debt 1990–2005, in Mozambique, Tanzania, Uganda and Zambia, in millions of US$ (source: World Bank, Global Development Finance online, 2007).

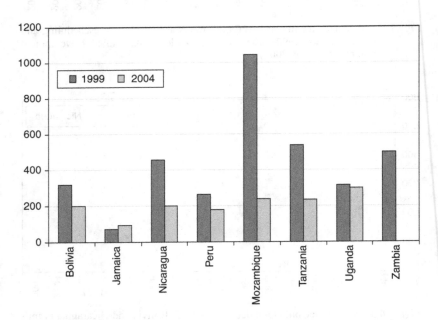

Figure 6.7 Debt/export ratios in the eight countries, (No data on exports available for Zambia in 2004) 1999 (Figures for 1999 may deviate slightly from those in Figure 4.5: in that case earlier export and/or debt data for 1999 have been adjusted in the Global Development Finance database) and 2004, in per cent (source: World Bank, Global Development Finance on-line, 2007).

figure was above the 150 per cent limit of the HIPC initiative. For the other HIPCs, the ratios vary between 200 and 240 per cent, which may or may not be below the 150 NPV target.

In sum, and looking at the six HIPCs followed in this book, the HIPC initiative has reduced debt stocks significantly and debt relief has freed resources to a much larger extent than during the 1990s. Nevertheless, external debt service did not decline in all HIPCs, and although debt sustainability improved, it is not clear whether it has improved sufficiently in order to make external debts sustainable.

Other evaluations of the HIPC initiative to date have also pointed to some limitations and problems (IDA 1999; OED 2003; Cohen *et al.* 2004; UNCTAD 2004; IEG 2006). While the original objective of HIPC was to achieve a permanent exit from debt rescheduling, by 2003 the objective was already formulated more modestly as 'Removing the debt overhang within a reasonable amount of time and providing a base from which to achieve debt sustainability and exit the rescheduling cycle' (World Bank and IMF Progress Report on HIPC, cited in IEG 2006). In fact, debt sustainability has only been achieved in a small number of countries.

On the one hand, this is due to the fact that eight years after the start of the initiative, almost half of the eligible countries still have not reached their decision point (ten countries) or completion point (eight countries). Several of the pre-decision point countries are or have been suffering from civil wars or armed cross-border conflicts (Eritrea, Liberia, Somalia and Sudan) (IDA and IMF 2006). All except Sudan have prepared or are in the process of preparing a Poverty Reduction Strategy Paper (PRSP) or an interim-PRSP. The most important bottleneck in all countries is the lack of an International Monetary Fund (IMF) agreement or, in one case (Nepal), the lack of satisfactory progress on an IMF agreement. Five countries have arrears with multilateral institutions. These have to be cleared first before the IMF is willing to discuss a new IMF agreement. The countries that are in the interim period between decision and completion point usually have a problem with macro-economic management, with implementing the required structural reforms or with developing a full PRSP with broad-based participation. In practice, the first one is dominant: countries have problems in meeting the IMF targets. And while, in principle, multilateral donors begin providing debt relief in the interim period, they are not obliged to do so and will frequently interrupt this in case of the country being off track. As a consequence, the country has even more problems in meeting the IMF targets.

On the other hand, even countries that fully benefited from the HIPC initiative after reaching the completion point did not achieve full debt sustainability (IEG 2006). In 11 out of 13 countries for which this could be established by the IEG evaluation, NPV of debt-to-export ratios have deteriorated since completion point. On average, these ratios increased (deteriorated) from 142 to 174 per cent. There are three major causes for this negative trend in debt sustainability.

First, not all non-Paris Club bilateral creditors co-operate with the initiative and the situation is worse for commercial creditors (IDA and IMF 2006). Nicaragua has the largest amount of non-Paris Club bilateral creditors of all HIPCs, 23, and has only been able to reach agreements with 12 of them, accounting for 40 per cent of debt relief expected from this group of creditors. One government has started litigation against Nicaragua. Many other HIPCs are affected by non-co-operation and litigation from commercial creditors. Commercial creditors account for 4 per cent of total debt relief of the 29 HIPCs that reached decision point and only 5.5 per cent of this has actually been provided. International Development Association (IDA) and IMF set out a survey among HIPCs, and 11 out of the 24 countries that responded proved to have experienced litigation from a total of 44 creditors. In 26 cases, the creditors won, costing about US$30 billion to several HIPCs, while 14 cases are still pending. These problems hamper debt sustainability for several countries, and they also lead to the continuation of uncertainty on future debt payments.

Second, export revenues have in many cases lagged behind expectations. Projections on future growth of income, exports and revenues were often set too optimistically. In fact, in the late 1990s when the debt sustainability analyses were carried out, primary export prices were at a rather high level, and they have fallen since then. Several countries have also suffered from large fluctuations in export prices. Third, the higher than projected debt-to-export ratios are caused by abundant new loans. For Bolivia and Uganda, this factor turns out to explain 30 and 38 per cent of the increase in the debt/export ratio since achieving completion point in 2001 (IEG 2006).

New loan disbursements

The abundant flow of new loans proved to be another reason for the limited relevance of debt relief in the 1990s. These new loans were mainly due to the fact that the most important lenders, in particular the IFIs, did not suffer the consequences of their bad loans. With the HIPC initiative, the IFIs themselves for the first time are contributing to the costs of debt relief. Theoretically, this could have put a halt to the moral hazard of the IFIs, so reducing the flow of new loans. However, closer inspection of the way in which the HIPC initiative is financed reveals that the greater part of debt relief from the IFIs is provided by bilateral donors.

For the World Bank, total costs of HIPC are estimated at US$12.5 billion in end-2005 NPV terms (IDA and IMF 2006). Apart from an initial contribution out of profits made on its loans to middle-income countries,[3] these costs are and will be financed from bilateral contributions on a pay-as-you-go basis, in the framework of the contributions to the IDA Replenishment Fund. In IDA 14 (covering fiscal years 2006–2008), the bilateral contributions committed amounted to US$1.4 billion, and in IDA 15 (covering fiscal years 2009–2011), it is estimated that US$2.2 billion is necessary for compensating non-forthcoming IDA reflows as a result of HIPC (IDA 2007). Most debt relief provided by the African Development Bank (AfDB) and the Inter-American Development Bank is also financed by bilateral donors, initially through a HIPC Trust Fund managed by the World Bank but also by donor promises to refund the soft loan windows of these banks.

The situation for the IMF is different because loans have a much shorter maturity period. The IMF needed a larger amount up front to cover the costs of debt relief and cannot rely in the same way on future donor contributions. Financing of the US$3.1 billion already provided or committed to countries that have reached completion point and decision point has already been secured. Donor contributions to a Poverty Reduction Strategy Facility (PRGF)–HIPC Trust Fund played a role, but a larger part was financed from 'off-market' gold sales.[4] However, total costs of the HIPC initiative for the IMF are estimated at US$5.6 billion in end-2005 NPV terms (IDA and IMF 2006). The financing of the remaining US$2.5 billion HIPC debt relief to pre-decision point countries still needs to be provided. It is likely that bilateral donors will be called upon to make additional contributions to the PRGF–HIPC Trust Fund.

In practice, the flow of new loans to the HIPCs has not stopped in 1999, and the overwhelming majority of new disbursements is provided by multilateral institutions. This was already the case in the 1990s but has since become even more significant (Figure 6.8). For the six HIPCs, this share has been between 86 (Nicaragua) and 95 per cent (Uganda). It has diminished for the non-HIPCs, Jamaica and Peru.

These trends in HIPCs are confirmed by the other evaluations of the initiative. As noted already in the early Operations Evaluation Department (OED) Review of the Initiative (2003), the problem already begins with a proliferation of objectives. While the first HIPC in 1996 focused on removing the debt overhang, the enhanced HIPC initiative also aimed at promoting growth and releasing resources for higher social spending to achieve poverty reduction. In order to achieve the latter, HIPC debt relief should be additional to regular aid. In practice, and given shrinking global aid budgets between 1996 and 2003, this meant that HIPCs would

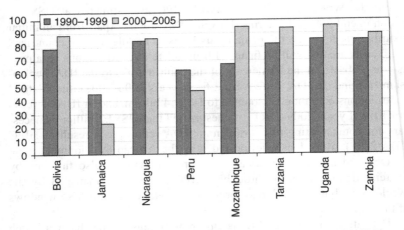

Figure 6.8 Share of multilateral creditors in new public loans, 1990–1999 and 2000–2005 (source: World Bank. Global Development Finance online, 2007).

probably receive more aid (including debt relief) than other low-income countries (OED 2003). The more recent evaluations conclude that indeed net flows to HIPCs have experienced larger growth than flows to other countries (Cohen *et al.* 2004; IEG 2006).

This has secured additionality for this particular group of countries, but it has several negative consequences. First, it affects the aid allocation since other low-income countries with possibly more urgent needs and better policies receive less aid than HIPCs. Second, and to the extent that new flows to HIPCs consisted of new loans, it has also perpetuated the debt problems of these countries and led to the need for further debt relief. Third, the continuation of new loans to HIPCs continued the inefficient use of bilateral grant money. Bilateral grant money is still used both to finance multilateral loans and to finance the forgiveness on the same loans. So far, these consequences imply a continuation of the problems of the international aid and debt architecture that were already observed during the 1990s. But the HIPC initiative added a fourth consequence. It led to redistribution between multilateral creditors and bilateral donors: maintaining the flow of new multilateral loans implies that an ever greater part of bilateral grant money be directed to the multilateral institutions. Whether this is positive or negative depends on one's judgment on the relative effectiveness of aid from the different channels.

Conditionality

A third reason why debt relief provided in the 1990s was not relevant proved to be the attached conditionality. It is therefore important to analyse the changes in conditionality that the enhanced HIPC initiative brought about. Before the HIPC initiative, all low- and middle-income countries with unsustainable debt could request debt relief from official creditors united in the Paris Club. The only condition for granting debt relief was that there should be an agreement with IMF regarding structural adjustment. HIPC, on the other hand, entails much stricter definitions of eligibility: countries must be poor (qualifying for IDA-only loans from the World Bank) and they must be heavily indebted, that is, have a NPV debt-to-export ratio of more than 150 per cent (or, in some cases, a debt-to-revenue ratio of more than 250 per cent). Chapter 2 above described that in order to reach the decision point of the enhanced HIPC initiative, eligible countries must not only have an agreement with the IMF but also elaborate a strategy for reducing poverty (PRSP) with civil society participation. In order to reach the completion point, they must remain on track with the IMF program for at least a year, must implement the PRSP for at least a year and must usually carry out a number of structural reforms.

As a result, the conditions for debt relief *became far more extensive* than they were in the 1990s. And, while the original HIPC initiative (1996) focused on 'ex post' conditions (requiring the successful completion of two successive three-year IMF adjustment programmes), the enhanced HIPC combines 'ex post' conditions (for completion point) with extensive 'ex ante' conditionality for the decision point. In view of the fact that, in roughly the same period, broad consensus was reached in academic circles (Killick *et al.* 1998; Collier *et al.* 1997) that it was useless to draw up conditions 'ex ante' and better to apply selectivity ('ex post'), this is a possibly unintended but nevertheless almost absurd development. It is also clear that the IMF still plays a central role in this conditionality: having an IMF agreement is necessary to reach decision point and completion point of the initiative.

Another change that came about with the HIPC initiative is that the IMF changed the name of its programme for the IDA-only countries, from Enhanced Structural Adjustment Facility (ESAF) to PRGF. This was supposed to be more than a name change: from then on, the IMF would make its programme compatible with the PRSP: a PRGF arrangement would be conditional on the existence of a PRSP that would have to be endorsed by executive boards of IMF and World Bank, and IMF conditions would be set in such a way that the country could implement its poverty reduction strategy.[5] The first of these implies that in fact, cross-conditionality would increase: not only would policy-based loans from multilateral development banks be dependent on an IMF programme, as before, but a concessional IMF programme (PRGF) would also be conditional upon a PRSP. This brought about heavier conditionality by the IFIs or, in other words, more extensive weight and power of the IFIs in the international aid architecture.

In the following, the effects of these changes will be examined, in particular in the four areas identified in this book as causes for the lack of relevance of debt relief: uncertainty for debtor countries, lack of implementation of conditions, lack of selectivity and even adverse selection and inappropriateness of conditions.

Uncertainty

For the (as of March 2007) 21 countries that did achieve completion point and that managed to conclude bilateral agreements with Paris Club members and other creditors, uncertainty on a substantial part of debt payments has come to an end. However, the extensive conditions for HIPC debt relief are the main reason that many countries that are in principle eligible for the initiative have not yet reached the decision point or completion point. For these countries, uncertainty on debt payments continues.

Ineffectiveness

The second problematic issue of conditionality, and especially conditionality 'ex ante', is that it is not very effective. Governments only implement what they already intended to implement. In the optimistic climate around the launching of the enhanced HIPC initiative, it was expected that the requirement to elaborate a PRSP would initiate a new phase of conditionality that would be completely different from earlier, traditional conditionality. It was expected that there would be a high degree of 'ownership' of PRSPs as countries would draw up their own strategies, and this ownership would be broad-based since they would do so in consultation with stakeholders. The idea was that conditionality would only be focussed on processes, not on contents. Donors would monitor only whether a PRSP exists and whether it had been elaborated in a participatory way. This was reflected in the formal procedure: the final documents would not have to be 'approved' but just 'endorsed' by the executive boards of World Bank and IMF. Yet, at the same time, PRSPs had to be the basis for a PRGF, they had to provide a policy framework for an increase in poverty reduction expenditure and they were also seen as the basis for aid in general.

There was scepticism on the feasibility of these PRSP objectives from the start, and this scepticism was later also confirmed in empirical studies. First, it is doubtful that process conditionality would be more effective than contents conditionality (Molenaers and Renard 2003). Donor attempts to influence domestic political processes have been shown to be particularly unsuccessful (Crawford 1997). Governments that do not really want participation can be expected to just organize cosmetic consultation and participation processes in order to get the debt relief. Second, the supposed focus on 'process conditionality' was not credible given that PRSPs were also the basis for a PRGF, for all other aid and for securing an increase in poverty reduction expenditure. Governments first and foremost seek approval of their strategies (no matter whether the word 'endorsed' is used) in order to get debt relief, and this undermines domestic ownership as well as any possible real attempts at participation. Limited ownership also means that governments will draw up a PRSP even if they are not interested in poverty reduction but will then do little to actually implement it. Third, it was often forgotten that traditional conditionality in the form of having an IMF agreement and, for completion point, carrying out the usual structural reforms was still in place.

This tension between ownership and conditionality has now been recognized and observed in PRSP reviews of the IMF and the World Bank themselves (IEO 2004; OED 2004). The six HIPCs followed in this book also provide some illustrations of the problems and tensions. In all countries, the governments have organized consultation meetings and, perhaps for the first time, have listened to representatives of non-governmental organizations (NGOs) and of the poor themselves. But these processes were often of a cosmetic nature. In Tanzania, participating NGOs did not receive the documentation in time to prepare well. In Nicaragua, consultation meetings were held so late that the results could not be incorporated in the PRSP. In Mozambique, local NGOs were aware only too well of the need for debt relief that it made them reluctant to bring forward their own position on poverty reduction. In all countries, NGOs complain that very little has been done with their inputs: when it came to the actual drawing up of the strategy, the government listened much more to the opinions of the donors and in particular the multilateral institutions than to those of civil society.

There are also doubts on the extent of national ownership of the strategy in these countries. In Nicaragua, it was clear to all donors that the administration directing the drawing up of the PRSP in 2001 was corrupt and not very interested in poverty reduction. Yet, the full PRSP was approved just before legislative and presidential elections, due to the political interests of one or two donors. In Mozambique and Tanzania, high government officials gave a higher priority (than in Nicaragua) to the fight against poverty, but this was not always the case among lower ranks in government institutions. Nicaragua had to comply with many structural reforms in order to reach completion point in 2004, including parliamentary approval of new social security laws that were against its Constitution. Parliament did so, but once completion point was reached, parliament did not approve further operational measures necessary to carry out the new laws. This confirms cosmetic implementation of the required conditions and thus lack of ownership.

Adverse selection

The third reason why conditions attached to debt relief did not promote the relevance of debt relief is the fact that they led to less selectivity, not only for debt relief itself but also for aid allocation in general. The institutional mechanism for this to happen proved to be the fact that IMF and World Bank prefer to lend to countries with high multilateral debts. The IMF is at the same time creditor and gatekeeper. Once there is an IMF agreement, a new flow of multilateral and bilateral programme aid comes about with which multilateral debt service can be paid. For the years before the HIPC initiative, it was already found that countries with higher multilateral debt received more aid and also that countries with worse policies received more aid (Birdsall *et al.* 2003). Easterly (2002) established that there was a direct relationship between bad policies and high levels of indebtedness. The question is whether the HIPC initiative, by reducing multilateral debts and making them more sustainable, has made an end to this adverse selection in the aid allocation.

However, the first evaluations are not very positive on this issue. The request for additionality for the HIPCs has led to higher inflows of both grants and loans for the HIPCs as compared to other low-income countries. This has raised concerns about the selectivity in the aid allocation (OED 2003; Killick 2004). Cohen *et al.* (2004) not only found that HIPCs received more aid (including debt relief) than other low-income countries, but also that highly indebted countries tended to have worse policies [measured by the Country Policy and Institutional Index (CPIA)] and lower levels of poverty [measured by their Human Development Index (HDI) rank]. The latter relationship was not very significant, however. These authors seem to conclude on a kind of path dependency in the aid allocation: given the quest for additionality and shrinking overall aid budgets, the HIPC initiative did not reduce the adverse selection.

Depetris Chauvin and Kraay (2006) examine the selectivity of aid and debt relief among a group of 62 low-income countries from 1989 to 2003. While they find that in the first five-year period (1989–1993) countries with worse policies (measured by the CPIA) received more aid and more debt relief, this was reversed in the last (1999–2003). Countries with better policies received more aid and more debt relief – especially more multilateral debt relief. This seems to indicate that selectivity in the aid allocation has improved since 1999. However, they also find that over time, debt relief has been given consistently to the same group of low-income countries. It is not influenced by within-country variations in growth, arrears accumulation or policies. In addition, there proves to be a relation between the size of the multilateral debtor (in terms of the multilateral debt-to-export ratio) and the granting of multilateral debt relief, indicating defensive granting of debt relief especially by the multilateral institutions. On the whole, they conclude along with Easterly (2002) that persistent country characteristics cause both high debts and large amounts of debt relief. In this conclusion, they ignore their finding of the increased selectivity of aid and multilateral debt relief.

However, an alternative explanation for these findings is possible. Since 1999, the CPIA has been more explicitly used for the allocation of World Bank (IDA) loans, so the increased selectivity of aid allocation if measured by CPIA is not very surprising. Several bilateral donors also began to follow the World Bank's CPIA score in their aid allocation. Given that CPIA scores are subjectively made by World Bank staff in the countries concerned, it can be expected that countries admitted to the decision point of the HIPC initiative get better CPIA scores (than before and than other countries) irrespective of whether policies have actually improved – just for the sake of consistency with the HIPC decision. In a way, the World Bank is now combining gatekeeper and creditor functions. As creditor, it has an interest in higher CPIA scores. HIPCs therefore get more debt relief (by definition), better CPIA scores and thus more new IDA loans.[6] In these countries, the debt problems continue because new World Bank loans perpetuate the debt problems, requiring new debt relief in the future.

Therefore, it might be the case that the underlying problem is not on the demand side: the persistent negative country characteristics causing both debt relief and new IFI loans, but on the supply side. The continued flow of new loan disbursements causes both continued debt problems and a need for more debt relief. As long as IMF and World Bank combine their role as gatekeepers and creditors for low-income countries, debt problems will continue and selectivity in the aid allocation will be reduced.

Contents of conditions

A fourth reason why conditionality was not beneficial for promoting growth through debt relief was that conditions were not always appropriate. Some of the conditions for the HIPC initiative are similar to those for earlier debt relief, such as requiring an IMF agreement and carrying out a set of structural reforms. However, with the introduction of HIPC and PRSP processes, it was also announced that the IMF would change in the sense of adjusting its policy recommendations to the existing PRSP and assessing beforehand the social and poverty consequences of its recommended policies. In practice, however, IMF operations have not changed. As the IEO (2007) of the IMF concluded, there is a wide gap between the rhetoric of the policy changes within the IMF and its operational activities at the country level. This means that traditional conditionality prevails – with all its risks as to the promotion of growth and poverty reduction.

For the World Bank, the PRSP process also implied a change in its structural adjustment loans. Its policy-based IDA loans are now called Poverty Reduction Strategy Credits (PRSC). The money is received by the Treasury, but its conditions cover a wide range of sectors, from public financial management through energy, water and communication to social security and health and education. In fact, the World Bank applies micro-management on a scale as never seen before, most of the conditions being of a process nature (requiring specific policies and measures) and at a very detailed level. In addition, and since PRSPs are usually not sufficiently operational, they bear little relationship with the contents of the (supposedly) nationally owned PRSP (Dijkstra 2006). As with the IMF, it implies a huge and continued risk of doing harm.

In addition to this old conditionality, there is now the new conditionality of the elaboration of a PRSP, with participation of civil society, and the requirement of a one-year implementation of a PRSP (for completion point). In practice, one of the conditions for completion point is also that the country can show an increase in poverty reduction expenditure as share in total government expenditure. This was all meant to guarantee that the resources freed by debt relief would be used for poverty reduction.

It can be questioned whether these conditions are appropriate. Evaluations already showed some unintended and sometimes negative effects (IEO 2004; OED 2004). The requirement of participation has induced governments to listen to civil society organizations, and sometimes for the first time. But the actual influence of people and representatives of organizations that participated in the consultations has remained small. The process was often not well thought out: it is almost impossible to discuss everything with everybody in a meaningful way and to draw conclusions from these meetings. In practice, the donors played a dominant role, and the legally elected representatives of the population, the members of parliaments, were often forgotten in the process. In this sense, the requirement of participation may even have done harm to domestic democratic processes.

As regards the contents of the strategies, it has been recognized that they focus too much on the social sectors and too little on how economic growth could be promoted and what its sources would be (IEG 2006). Issues of distribution (of land, of income, by ethnic group and by gender) were also generally neglected. It can therefore be doubted whether implementation of the strategies will lead to economic growth and to sustainable poverty reduction. The bias towards promoting the social sectors is reinforced by the practice of tracking 'poverty reducing spending' within total public expenditure. In fact, poverty reducing expenditure has increased in the 29 HIPCs that had reached decision point from 7 per cent of gross domestic product (GDP) in 1999 to 9 per cent in 2005 (IDA and IMF 2006). Definitions of poverty reduction expenditure vary between countries and often also over time, but the social sectors education and health always occupy a large component. Despite this increased social sector spending in most countries, results in terms of social indicators and poverty reduction are mixed. Some indicators seem to have improved (access to primary education), while others, such as maternal mortality rates and reduction of infectious diseases, have not (IEG 2006).

The more recent poverty reduction strategies give more attention to growth, but the quality varies and in practice most attention is still given to government spending instead of integrating, as the IEG evaluation concludes, '...the full range of policy actions required for poverty reduction' (IEG 2006). In addition, they still give priority to social services and much less to infrastructure for productive purposes.

However, it is not clear what the 'full range of policy actions required for poverty reduction' is, and governments of HIPCs probably assume that donors are nowadays more interested in the social sectors in view of the Millennium Development Goals than in physical infrastructure. With respect to measures that may overcome productive bottlenecks, such as subsidized credit, fertilizers or other interventions in the market, they can be almost sure that these type of measures will not be accepted by World Bank and IMF and will lead to the rejection of the PRSP – despite the fact that such measures are very common in the industrialized countries and in countries such as Brazil, China and India that are much less dependent on aid and on agreements with the IFIs.

Given the problems and possible future problems of the contents of the conditions, it can be questioned whether conditions should be put for debt relief at all. In addition to possible inadequacies, there is also a moral issue. Creditors have set conditions in the past, either in the form of projects that had to be carried out or in the form of policies to be implemented. Given the unsustainability of the debts of these countries, conditions apparently have not been the right ones. Arguably, creditors and donors may have a say in their aid operations in the first instance, but they lose this influence once their conditions have proven wrong and debt write-offs are necessary.

Combining this conclusion of possible inappropriate conditions with that on the supply side as cause for perpetuating debt problems in some low-income countries, one can even wonder whether these countries would not be better off without new programmes of the IFIs. It is not just the supply of new *loans* that causes persistent problems, but the continuous supply of new and possibly inappropriate conditions as well.

Recent changes in international aid and debt architecture and prospects for the future

In 2004, the World Bank and the IMF developed a new DSF. In their debt sustainability analysis, they now take into account the quality of policy and institutions measured by the Bank's Country Policy and Institutional Assessment (CPIA). The framework is based on empirical work showing that the risk of 'debt distress'[7] depends on the debt burden itself, the quality of policy and institutions and external shocks as reflected in GDP growth (Kraay and Nehru 2003). The new forward looking debt sustainability analyses of IDA and IMF take indicators for external and public debt (including domestic debt) into account as well as realistic assumptions for exogenous shocks and past scores on the CPIA. In addition to providing an improved capacity for analysing the debt situation of low-income countries, the new DSF also plays a role in the allocation of IDA resources.

In the context of IDA 14 (covering fiscal years 2006–2008), it was decided that up to 30 per cent of IDA resources could be provided as grants instead of (soft) loans.[8] For the allocation of total IDA resources to low-income countries, the CPIA remains decisive. But the new DSF plays a role in this allocation. Countries that have a higher risk of debt distress, as measured by a higher NPV debt-to-export ratio and a lower score on the CPIA, receive a larger amount of grants instead of loans. However, to the extent they receive grants, they are 'punished' with a 20 per cent discount. Part of this discount (11 per cent of the total grant amount) is redistributed among all IDA recipients; the other part is compensation for IDA for the reduced IDA reflows.

The fact that more IDA resources are now provided as grants is positive since it leads to a lower future debt burden for low-income countries. It will reduce the problem that highly indebted countries continue receiving loans. However, in the current situation, countries with higher debts and worse policies receive more grants – albeit with a discount of 20 per cent of the total quantity. This implies rewarding countries for their 'bad behaviour'. In addition, the fact that most IDA resources are still provided as loans is likely to perpetuate the debt problems of low-income countries.

Under British presidency of the G8, the July 2005 summit at Gleneagles decided to give further debt relief to the HIPCs, with the aim of better helping them to achieve the Millennium Development Goals. This proposal was later elaborated by staffs of IDA and IMF into the MDRI and as such approved by the boards of the institutions. It entailed 100 per cent debt forgiveness on all pre-2005 debts to IMF and AfDB and all pre-2004 debts to the World Bank. Countries that had reached completion point were eligible for MDRI provided there were no signs of deterioration in performance with respect to macro-economic stability or the implementation of their PRSP. In practice, in 2006, all countries that had reached completion point of HIPC received the 100 per cent cancellation. It was agreed that from then on, MDRI would be provided automatically to countries reaching their HIPC completion point. The IMF began to apply this MDRI in January 2006 and the World Bank in July 2006.

In practice, the MDRI implies a large amount of additional debt relief for the limited group of countries that had already received a large amount of debt relief. Since for most HIPCs, multilateral loans were the largest component of new debts since the 1990s, this reduces their external debt service burden considerably. There is no new conditionality involved beyond the conditions for the HIPC initiative. This implies that the possible adverse selection induced by the HIPC initiative is extended to the selection of recipients for the MDRI. However, for the group of countries benefiting from MDRI, multilateral debts have disappeared which means that from now on, more selectivity in the aid allocation can be applied to these countries. Defensive lending or defensive granting is not necessary anymore – at least, in the short term.

However, the possible effects of the MDRI also depend on how this initiative is financed. In practice, bilateral donors have committed to compensate the IFIs fully for the costs involved, estimated at US$50 billion for the three institutions over 40 years.[9] In the case of the IMF, financing of the debt cancellation is expected to be covered from the PRGF–HIPC Trust Fund which depends on contributions from donor countries. In the case of the World Bank, costs are estimated at US$37 billion over 40 years, and the donors have committed to cover these costs on a pay-as-you-go basis through their contributions to the IDA Replenishment Fund. Similarly, donor contributions are also expected to maintain the resources of the soft loan window of the AfDB.

This financing of the MDRI implies that there is a continued risk of moral hazard. To the extent that these institutions continue to extend loans and as long as they do not suffer the consequences of their lending themselves, they are likely to extend higher volumes of loans than necessary or beneficial for the recipient countries. This way of financing also implies that the inefficient allocation of bilateral grant money continues. In fact, all loans from IMF, World Bank and AfDB to this group of countries have actually become grants. One can therefore ask the question why these institutions do not provide grants in the first place. The extensive donor commitments to compensate these institutions for foregone reflows or repayments also imply that the redistribution between bilateral donors and multilateral institutions continues. Given that aid budgets are fixed (for example, in terms of GDP) or in any case determined irrespective of specific commitments to multilateral institutions, these commitments imply that bilateral grant money to developing countries is substituted for new multilateral loans. History has learnt that these loans have dubious consequences for debt sustainability and in fact also for growth and development.

The IMF and the World Bank themselves are concerned that the combination of the HIPC, the MDRI and the DSF will lead to new indebtedness from other, perhaps less concessional creditors such as China or other emerging economies (World Bank and IMF 2006). They would be able to free ride on the debt forgiveness provided by the multilateral institutions. However, to the extent that this is the case, it should be seen as an indicator for success of the measures taken to achieve debt sustainability: countries regain access to new loans from other bilateral and commercial creditors. It is possible that these new creditors are more successful in their lending allocations, in terms of promoting growth of income and exports, than the multilateral institutions have been. If not, so if these countries would not be able to repay these debts, the new creditors will be responsible and they should (partially) write off these bad loans. The current attempts of IMF and World Bank to punish countries that engage in new loans from other creditors with harsher conditions and lower aid volumes indicate an attempt to retain and even extend control over the HIPCs, while at the same time denying them chances of development. In principle, there is nothing against selectivity in the aid allocation decision, but it appears now to be applied for the wrong reasons.

It is much more likely that the IFIs themselves will again free ride on the debt relief financed by bilateral donors, in which case adverse selection also continues: HIPCs that do not have access to loans from other creditors (so possibly have worse policies) will receive more new disbursements from the IFIs than HIPCs receiving loans from new creditors. And due to the application of the DSF, HIPCs with higher chances of debt distress due to worse policies will receive a higher share of grants within total IDA disbursements.

Conclusion

It is clear that after the enhanced HIPC initiative and especially after MDRI, the 21 countries that have fully benefited from these initiatives have obtained large reductions in the NPV of their debt stocks and in their debt service. With respect to amounts and modalities of debt relief, there are clear improvements as compared to the 1990s. However, the other two problematic issues of the aid and debt architecture that emerged as lessons from the analysis of the impact of debt relief in this book are still largely unresolved.

First, and given that both HIPC and MDRI multilateral debt relief is mainly financed from bilateral grant money, the IFIs still experience moral hazard. They do not bear the consequences of risky lending themselves, and this tends to lead to a continuous flow of new loan disbursements. This was particularly evident after the enhanced HIPC initiative, with multilateral loans making up between 86 and 95 per cent of the new loans of the six HIPCs followed in this book. These new multilateral loans were an important factor behind the need for further debt relief. But the flow of multilateral loans will most likely continue today after the application of MDRI. The inefficient use of bilateral grant money has continued after HIPC as well and most likely will continue further. In practice, MDRI means that all loans from the IFIs to the HIPCs extended before 2004 (IDA) or before 2005 (IMF and AfDB) actually have become grants. This inefficient use of bilateral grant money, the moral hazard and the continuous flow of new loans leading to perpetuation of debt problems will only stop if all IDA loans become grants.

Second, conditionality for accession to the HIPC initiative (and thereby also for MDRI) is heavy and even heavier than in the 1990s. This implies that a large group of countries badly in need of debt relief (or debt write-offs) does not get it because they do not meet the conditions. The other problems related to conditionality are also still there: it is not always effective, so in those cases, conditionality implies a waste of time and resources, and the conditions may not be appropriate for growth and poverty reduction. This also gives rise to a moral problem with setting conditions for debt relief: the relief has become necessary due to inadequate conditions set by creditors and donors on extending the loan in the first place. Why would creditors have a right to set conditions again when they write off the same loan? Finally, conditionality may imply that adverse selection in the aid allocation continues, basically due to the fact that the IFIs continue to be gatekeepers for international concessional financing by setting the conditions for it, and at the same time have an interest in new loans.

However, for countries that benefited fully from HIPC and MDRI, it is in principle possible that the aid allocation improves: defensive lending or granting is no longer necessary and more aid can be directed to countries with good policies and good governance. But there are two forces working in the opposite direction of improved selectivity. First, the application of the new DSF leads to a higher grant share for countries with worse policies. This issue can easily be solved by deciding on 100 per cent IDA grants. Second, the World Bank and the IMF are considering sanctions in the form of more conditions and lower disbursements to HIPCs that have access to less concessional loans from new creditors, so possibly have better policies. In addition, this can be seen as an attempt by the IFIs to regain control over countries that have graduated from multilateral debt problems and thus have become less dependent on the IFIs with their conditionality. In this way, each new phase in the debt situation of poor countries seems to lead to more, not less conditionality by the IFIs. Countries enter in a vicious circle with continuous new multilateral loans and continuous dependence on the IFIs.

Easterly (2002, 2006) and Depetris Chauvin and Kraay (2005) have advanced the hypothesis that persistent debtor country characteristics lead to continuous involvement of the IFIs and continuous debt problems. This book draws attention to an alternative hypothesis: persistent involvement of the IFIs in the form of new loans and conditionality leads to a continuation of debt problems and to less adequate policies.

Notes

1 Introduction

1 The Millennium Development Goals include eight goals formulated by the international community, 18 targets and 48 indicators that were approved by the United Nations General Assembly in 2000. The most important goal is that (1) the number of people living in poverty (i.e. on less than US$1 per day) should be halved between 1990 and 2015. The other goals are (2) universal access to basic education, (3) the promotion of equality between men and women, (4) the reduction of child mortality, (5) the reduction of maternal mortality rates, (6) the combating of AIDS, malaria and other diseases, (7) ensuring a sustainable environment and (8) the encouragement of a world-wide partnership for development, to be expressed, for example, in increasing development aid to 0.7 per cent of GDP.

2 These studies are discussed in Chapter 5 of this book.

3 The NPV is the sum of all debt repayments and interest payments, discounted against the current market rate. If the actual interest is lower than the market rate (and/or the maturity is longer and/or there is a longer grace period), the NPV of a debt is lower than its nominal value. In view of the fact that many HIPC debts are concessional, i.e. they have a lower interest rate and/or longer maturity and/or grace periods, the NPV of those debts is lower than the nominal value.

4 See, for example, Cohen (1993), Elbadawi *et al.* (1997) and other studies, discussed in Chapter 5 of this book.

5 Analogous to the Laffer curve in fiscal theory: when the tax rate reaches a certain level, tax revenue will no longer increase but decrease, due to declining efforts by (taxable) income-earners as well as to tax avoidance and evasion.

6 Based on estimates of secondary market prices of debt claims, Claessens concluded that five countries were on the downward part of the debt Laffer curve, including four of those discussed in this study: Bolivia, Nicaragua, Peru and Zambia.

7 This is especially a problem since 2000, because debt relief on multilateral debts in the context of the HIPC initiative is given as relief on debt service flows, and this debt service to multilateral banks would have been paid anyway. This makes the ratio debt service paid/debt service due less suitable as indicator for debt overhang since 2000.

2 The origins of debt and an overview of debt relief

1 Named after the then Secretary of the US Treasury James Baker.
2 The Paris Club is an informal club of official bilateral creditors that deals with the payment difficulties of debtor nations in a co-ordinated way. It has existed since 1956.
3 According to an IMF (2001) study, Mozambique started to borrow at the end of the 1970s, particularly from East European countries. These loans are not recorded in the World Bank's data bank, however.
4 This was partly because much bilateral aid then consisted of grants and no longer of loans.
5 Between 1979 and 1982, the transition took place from a military dictatorship to a democratically elected government.
6 Usually, it was only possible to trace the Dutch contribution. Figures regarding contributions by other donors were sometimes found during the field studies but proved not to tally with regard to the Netherlands. The fifth dimension was applied until about 1996, i.e. before the World Bank became more transparent and Internet began to be used.
7 The amounts of debt relief received by the eight countries since 1999 are shown in Chapter 6.
8 However, it is reflected in the IMF's balance-of-payments figures.
9 Recipient countries were expected to use MDF contributions to pay the debt service to multilateral institutions. In view of the fact that they would otherwise have had to pay from their own resources, this released monies that were known as 'countervalue funds', analogous to countervalue funds generated by import support. Bilateral donors who contributed to an MDF frequently demanded that these funds be used for specific purposes such as the social sectors.

3 The efficiency of debt relief

1 See note c, Table 3.1.
2 In view of the fact that export credit (guarantee) agencies usually belong to the government or operate on its behalf, it is not strictly speaking a case of one party bailing out another.
3 This is done through contributions to the (interest) subsidy account of the IMF's ESAF–PRGF Trust, to the 'Replenishment Fund' of the IDA and to similar funds of the IDB and the African Development Bank.
4 This holds for all debt relief on multilateral debts and on bilateral commercial debts (the debts to the ECAs) as well as for relief on interest payments on bilateral (concessional) aid loans. Debt relief on the principal of bilateral aid loans does not qualify, in principle, as ODA. The mechanism is that the debt relief on ODA loans is included, but there is an offsetting flow in the form of a hypothetical amortization payment. However, if and to the extent that amortizations on these loans would have been paid in the absence of debt relief, this debt relief also leads to additional ODA: without the relief, net ODA would have been smaller.
5 Another, more general problem with this article is that it is not clear how 'debt relief' or 'debt forgiveness' has been defined and from what source the data are taken.
6 This was not always the case at the start of the 1990s, however. In Bolivia,

Nicaragua and Zambia, roughly two-thirds of outstanding multilateral debt was still non-concessional in 1990.

7 In 1995 and 1999, the IMF was unable to provide a second tranche because targets had not been met; however, the IMF representative asked other donors to continue their programme aid.

8 When the condition that a PRSP be completed on a participatory basis proved too difficult for many countries, so that in 2000 a number threatened to fall by the wayside, the entry requirement to the decision point was toned down to formulating an *interim* PRSP that had the character of a draft strategy. This revision was successful in that by 31 December 2000, 22 HIPCs had qualified for the decision point. In Washington, the phenomenon became known as the 'Millennium rush'.

4 The effectiveness of debt relief

1 These obligations included payments on claims that had been restructured during the 1980s.

2 A 'push' factor also played a role in the new inflow, namely lower interest rates in the USA (Dooley *et al.* 1994; Hernández and Rudolph 1995).

3 According to another study, the accumulated amount of flight capital over a 25-year period until 1996, for 30 African countries, averaged 180 per cent of the annual GNP (Ndikumana and Boyce 2003:115).

4 The latter indicator has been added since low annual debt service payments may be due to high arrears and not to a healthy liquidity position. It will be dealt with in the next section, since it is also an indicator for debt overhang.

5 The inflow of new *official* capital could, in principle, also be seen as an indicator of increased creditworthiness. The inflow of new multilateral loans, however, is only held up if there are arrears with the IFIs themselves. Arrears with other creditors do not matter because the multilaterals are preferred creditors.

6 It may be expected that the net inflow of foreign direct investment will be less sensitive to the magnitude of foreign debt or to creditworthiness, because it does not involve loans that have to be repaid.

7 A maximum of 50 per cent of shares in former state companies have been transferred to pension funds that are entitled to sell their shares to private investors.

8 From, among others, the International Finance Corporation (IFC) of the World Bank Group.

9 These figures, like so many others, must be approached with caution. In Nicaragua, the under-valuing of GDP probably played a role in the large rise, while in Tanzania, the changed system of national accounting can probably explain part of the reduction. Although investments were high in Jamaica, the growth of GDP was very low. One explanation given for this 'growth paradox' is that GDP is underestimated and that figures for investments/GDP are therefore too high.

10 Aid and debt relief obviously only lead to equal amounts of extra imports as long as all other flows on the balance of payments remain constant, e.g. exports, the net inflow of capital, direct investment.

11 This does not imply automatically that real spending has also fallen. Conversely, actual expenditure on social sectors can decrease even if expenditure

rises as percentage of GDP. This is because wages and salaries represent the greater part of expenditure on the social sectors. If nominal wage costs rise more (less) than nominal GDP, actual expenditure on social sectors will increase less (more) than if calculated as percentage of GDP. This can cause considerable variations (see Botchwey *et al.* 1998).

12 The threshold value of 150 per cent is based on the NPV of the debt (see Annex 5). For countries with many concessional loans, a critical value of 150 per cent for the NPV debt/export will allow a somewhat higher ratio in nominal terms.

13 The export figures (GDF) used in columns 2–4 include income transfers from abroad (remittances). This seems justified given that such remittances finance part of the deficit.

14 ... or if the margin between export growth and interest rate does not become greater. The chance of this happening seems small, however, seeing that export growth in these countries was considerable during the 1990s; it is more likely that the margin will decrease, thus making it even more essential that the trade deficit should also decrease.

15 This 60 per cent is probably too high for low- and middle-income countries in view of the fact that they are financially far more vulnerable than developed countries. See Houben 2002.

16 According to another study, there is also a strong relationship between new loans *to* African countries and private capital flight *from* those countries: it is estimated that, for every dollar received in loans, 80 cents leave the country again in the form of private capital (Ndikumana and Boyce 2003).

17 Calculated on the basis of nominal dollar figures from the WDI database.

18 This certainly applied in the eight countries studied in this evaluation but also proved to be the case in the 18 programme countries of Swedish bilateral aid (see White and Dijkstra 2003).

19 For example, reductions of excessive budget deficits and liberalization of the foreign exchange markets have always been beneficial for economic growth.

20 That this was the incorrect sequence was put forth in 1993, e.g. by McKinnon (1993). The same mistakes have unfortunately been often repeated since then.

21 Meetings of representatives of donors and of the recipient country, usually held once yearly.

5 The relevance of debt relief

1 According to Kirkpatrick and Tennant (2002), the fall would have been much greater if the government had allowed the banks to go bankrupt. That would have undermined confidence in the financial sector and given rise to enormous capital flight.

2 In relation to exports or GDP, sometimes in year t, and sometimes in year $t-1$, both nominal debt and NPV of debt have been taken.

3 This method controls for endogeneity of possible explanatory variables. The lagged differences of the exogenous variables are used as instruments.

4 Presbitero (2005), for example, finds exactly this same difference between the OLS and the GMM methods.

5 The data represent ten-year averages; thus, there are only three observations (per country and per variable) and only one for the 1990s. The GMM requires a panel data set per period.

6 The coefficient of variation is the standard deviation divided by the mean.
7 In Zambia, earlier liberalization that had been prescribed by the IFIs has now been reversed, with positive effects on agricultural output.

6 The impact of debt relief since 2000 and prospects for the future

1 This cut-off date is country-specific but usually is much earlier than the date of the decision point. However, after this cut-off date for bilateral debt, most bilateral donors began to disburse only grants, and several bilateral creditors granted debt relief 'beyond HIPC', also covering more recent debts and/or topping up relief to 100 per cent of pre-cut-off date debts.
2 Nicaragua obtained very large stock reductions already in the mid-1990s (on former Soviet Union, former East German and Mexican debts, see Chapter 2).
3 This contribution amounted to US$2.2 billion in 1999, so the end-2005 NPV is somewhat higher.
4 At first, IMF planned to sell part of its gold reserves for the purpose, but this was objected to by the major gold-producing countries. The plan was then changed to 'off-market' gold sales, meaning that a quantity of gold is sold symbolically and then bought back in the framework of a transaction with a member state. This 'paper' sale and repurchase of gold enables its book value to be upgraded. The investment income on the proceeds of this upgrading has been used for the HIPC initiative.
5 This also applied to non-HIPCs.
6 They often also received more bilateral grants, either because bilaterals also used CPIA scores in their aid allocation decisions or because bilaterals decided to give more aid to HIPCs, assuming that these countries had been selected as a result of good policies. The latter happened in the UK, for example.
7 This is defined as a period in which countries have significant arrears, use Paris Club rescheduling or have a concessional agreement with the IMF (SAF, ESAF or PRGF).
8 In practice, the share of grants is lower. In its long-term projections, IDA (2007) assumes a grant share of 20 per cent.
9 'Multilateral Debt Relief Initiative MDRI Fact Sheet', www.worldbank.org/intdebtdept/resources.

Bibliography

Abdelgalil, E. and Cornelissen, W. (2003a) 'Results of international debt relief in Bolivia', The Hague, IOB, Working Document.
—— (2003b) 'Results of international debt relief in Jamaica', The Hague, IOB, Working Document.
—— (2003c) 'Results of international debt relief in Peru', The Hague, IOB, Working Document.
Acharya, S. and Diwan, I. (1993) 'Debt buybacks signal sovereign countries' creditworthiness: Theory and tests', International Economic Review, 34(4): 795–817.
Asiedu, E. (2003) 'Debt relief and institutional reform: A focus on heavily indebted poor countries', The Quarterly Review of Economics and Finance, 43: 614–26.
Berlage, L., Cassimon, D., Drèze, J. and Reding, P. (2003) 'Prospective aid and indebtedness relief: A proposal', World Development, 31(10): 1635–54.
Bhagwati, J.N. (2004) In defense of globalization, New York: Oxford University Press.
Bird, G. (2001) 'IMF programs: Do they work? Can they be made to work better?' World Development, 29(11): 1849–65.
Bird, G. and Rowlands, D. (2000) 'The catalyzing role of policy-based lending by the IMF and the World Bank: Fact or fiction?' Journal of International Development, 12(7): 951–73.
Birdsall, N. and Williamson, J. with Deese, B. (2002) Delivering on debt relief: From IMF gold to a new aid architecture, Washington, DC: Center for Global Development and Institute for International Economics.
Birdsall, N., Claessens, S. and Diwan, I. (2003) 'Policy selectivity forgone: Debt and donor behaviour in Africa', World Bank Economic Review, 17(3): 409–35.
Boehmer, E. and Megginson, W.L. (1990) 'Determinants of secondary market prices for developing country syndicated loans', The Journal of Finance, 45(6): 1517–40.
Bossema, W. (1995) Mozambique, Amsterdam/'s-Gravenhage: KIT/NOVIB/ NCOS.
Botchwey, K., Collier, P., Gunning, J.W. and Hamada, K. (1998) External evaluation of the ESAF, report by a group of independent experts, Washington, DC: IMF.
Bowe, M. and Dean, J.W. (1997) 'Has the market solved the sovereign debt

crisis?' Princeton, NJ, International Finance Section, Princeton University, Princeton Studies in International Finance No. 83.

Claessens, S. (1990) 'The debt Laffer curve: Some estimates', *World Development*, 18(12): 1671–7.

Claessens, S., Oks, D. and Van Wijnbergen, S. (1994) 'Interest rates, growth and external debt: The macroeconomic impact of Mexico's Brady deal', London, Centre for Economic Policy Research (CEPR), Discussion Paper No. 904.

Clements, B., Bhattacharya, R. and Quoc Nguyen, T. (2003) 'External debt, public investment and growth in low-income countries', Washington, DC, IMF Working Paper No. 03/249.

Cline, W.R. (1995) *International debt reexamined*, Washington, DC: Institute for International Economics.

Cohen, D. (1993) 'Low investment and large LDC debt in the 1980s', *American Economic Review*, 83(3): 437–49.

—— (1997) 'Growth and external debt: A new perspective on the African and Latin American tragedies', London, Centre for Economic Policy Research (CEPR), Discussion Paper No. 1753.

—— (2000) 'The HIPC initiative: True and false promises', London, Centre for Economic Policy Research (CEPR), Discussion Paper No. 2632.

Cohen, D., Phamtan, M., Rampulla, C. and Vellutini, C. (2004) 'Beyond the HIPC initiative', Paris, Investment Development Consultancy, Report commissioned by European Commission.

Collier, P., Guillaumont, P., Guillaumont, S. and Gunning, J.W. (1997) 'Redesigning conditionality', *World Development*, 25(9): 1399–407.

Collier, P., Hoeffler, A. and Pattillo, C. (2001) 'Flight capital as a portfolio choice', *World Bank Economic Review*, 15(1): 55–80.

Cordella, T., Ricci, L.A. and Ruiz-Arranz, M. (2005). 'Debt overhang or debt irrelevance? Revisiting the debt-growth link', Washington, DC, IMF Working Paper No. 05/223.

Corden, M. (1989) 'Debt relief and adjustment initiatives', in Frankel, J.A., Dooley, M. and Wickham, P. (eds) *Analytical issues on debt*, Washington, DC: International Monetary Fund: 242–57.

Crawford, G. (1997) 'Foreign aid and political conditionality: Issues of effectiveness and consistency', *Democratization*, 4(3): 69–108.

Danielson, A. and Dijkstra, G. (2003) 'Results of international debt relief in Tanzania', The Hague, IOB, Working Document.

Daseking, C. and Powell, R. (1999) 'From Toronto terms to the HIPC initiative: A brief history of debt relief to low-income countries', Washington, DC, IMF Working Paper No. 99/142.

Depetris Chauvin, N. and Kraay, A. (2005) 'What has 100 billion dollars worth of debt relief done for low-income countries?' Washington, DC, Mimeo.

—— (2006) 'Who gets debt relief?' Washington, DC, The World Bank, Policy Research Working Paper No. 4000.

Deshpande, A. (1997) 'The debt overhang and the disincentive to invest', *Journal of Development Economics*, 52: 169–87.

Dijkstra, A.G. (2002) 'The effectiveness of policy conditionality: Eight country experiences', *Development and Change*, 33(2): 307–34.

—— (2003) 'Results of international debt relief in Mozambique', The Hague, IOB, Working Document.

—— (2006) 'The PRS process and harmonization & alignment: Reflections on aid effectiveness', Antwerp, Paper presented to International Conference 'Challenging the Poverty Reduction Paradigm'.

Dijkstra, G. and Evans, T. (2003) 'Results of international debt relief in Nicaragua', The Hague, IOB, Working Document.

Dijkstra, G. and Hermes, N. (2003) 'The debt crisis, international responses, and results of debt relief: Report of a literature survey and an econometric analysis', The Hague, IOB, Working Document.

Dijkstra, A.G. and Van Donge, J.K. (2001) 'What does the "show case" show? Evidence of, and lessons from adjustment in Uganda', *World Development*, 29(5): 841–63.

Dollar, D. and Svensson, J. (2000) 'What explains the success or failure of structural adjustment programs?' *Economic Journal*, 110: 894–917.

Dollar, D., Devarajan, S. and Holmgren, T. (eds) (2001) *Aid and reform in Africa*, Washington, DC: The World Bank.

Dooley, M.P. (1994) 'A retrospective on the debt crisis', Washington, DC, NBER Working Paper No. 4963.

Dooley, M.P., Fernández-Arias, E. and Kletzer, K.M. (1994) 'Recent private capital inflows to developing countries: Is the debt crisis history?' Cambridge, MA, National Bureau of Economic Research (NBER) Working Paper No. 4792.

Dreher, A. (2004) 'A public choice perspective of IMF and World Bank lending and conditionality', *Public Choice* 119: 445–64.

—— (2006) 'IMF and economic growth: The effects of programs, loans, and compliance with conditionality', *World Development*, 34(5): 769–88.

Easterly, W. (2002) 'How did heavily indebted poor countries become heavily indebted? Reviewing two decades of debt relief', *World Development*, 30(10): 1677–96.

—— (2006) *The White men's burden: Why the West's efforts to aid the rest have done so much ill and so little good*, New York: The Penguin Press.

Elbadawi, I.A., Ndulu, B.J. and Ndung'u, N. (1997) 'Debt overhang and economic growth in sub-Saharan Africa', in Iqbal, Z. and Kanbur, R. (eds) *External finance for low-income countries*, Washington, DC: IMF: 49–76.

Gillis, M., Perkins, D.H., Roemer, M. and Snodgrass, D.R. (1996) *Economics of development*, 4th edn, New York/London: Norton.

Haggard, S. (1985) 'The politics of adjustment', *International Organization*, 39(3): 505–34.

Hanlon, J. (2000) 'How much debt must be cancelled?' *Journal of International Development*, 12(6): 877–901.

Hansen, H. (2004) 'The impact of external aid and external debt on growth and investment', in Addison, T., Hansen, H. and Tarp, F. (eds) *Debt relief for poor countries*, Basingstoke and New York: Palgrave Macmillan: 134–57.

Harrison, G. (2001) 'Post-conditionality politics and administrative reform: Reflections on the cases of Uganda and Tanzania', *Development and Change*, 32(4): 657–79.

Hernández, L. and Katada, S.N. (1996) 'Grants and debt forgiveness in Africa', Washington, DC, World Bank Policy Research Working Paper No. 1653.

Hernández, L. and Rudolph, H. (1995) 'Sustainability of private capital flows to developing countries: Is a general reversal likely?' Washington, DC, International Economics Department, The World Bank, Policy Research Working Paper No. 1518.

Hertz, N. (2004) *IOU: The debt threat and why we must defuse it*, London: Fourth Estate.

Houben, A. (2002) 'De ene schuld is de andere niet', *Economisch-Statistische Berichten*, 87(4384): 824–5.

IDA (1999) 'Tanzania: Grant from the debt reduction facility for IDA-only countries for a proposed debt reduction operation', Washington, DC, The World Bank IDA/R99–135.

—— (2007) 'IDA 15: IDA's long-term financial capacity', Washington, DC, Resource Mobilization (FRM).

IDA and IMF (2006) *HIPC initiative and MDRI initiative: Status of implementation*, Washington, DC.

IEG (2006) *Debt relief for the poorest: An evaluation update of the HIPC initiative*, Washington, DC: The World Bank.

IEO (2004) *IEO evaluation report on PRSPs and the PRGF*, Washington, DC: IMF.

—— (2007) *An evaluation of the IMF and aid to sub-Saharan Africa*, Washington, DC: IMF.

Imbs, J. and Ranciere, R. (2005) 'The overhang hangover', Washington, DC, World Bank Policy Research Working Paper No. WPS3673.

IMF (2001) *Republic of Mozambique: Selected issues and statistical appendix*, Washington, DC: 112.

Killick, T. (1995) *IMF programmes in developing countries: Design and impact*, London: Routledge.

—— (2004) 'Politics, evidence and the new aid agenda', *Development Policy Review*, 22(1): 5–29.

Killick, T., with Gunatilaka, R. and Marr, A. (1998) *Aid and the political economy of policy change*, London and New York: Routledge.

Kirkpatrick, C. and Tennant, D. (2002) 'Responding to financial crisis: The case of Jamaica', *World Development*, 30(11): 1933–50.

Kraay, A. and Nehru, V. (2003) *When is external debt sustainable?* Washington, DC: The World Bank.

Krugman, P.R. (1988) 'Financing versus forgiving a debt overhang', *Journal of Development Economics*, 29: 253–68.

Lensink, R. and Morrissey, O. (2000) 'Uncertainty of aid inflows and the aid-growth relationship', *Journal of Development Studies*, 36(3): 31–49.

Lindner, M. (2003a) 'Results of international debt relief in Uganda', The Hague, IOB, Working Document.

—— (2003b) 'Results of international debt relief in Zambia', The Hague, IOB, Working Document.

McKinnon, R.I. (1993) *The order of economic liberalization: Financial control in the transition economy*, Baltimore and London: Johns Hopkins University Press.

Marchesi, S. and Missale, A. (2004). 'What does motivate lending and aid to the HIPCs?' Siena/Milano, Paper presented to the conference Debt Relief and Global Governance, Rotterdam.

Molenaers, N. and Renard, R. (2003) 'The World Bank, participation and PRSP: The Bolivian case revisited', *European Journal of Development Research*, 15(2): 133–61.

Morisset, J. (1991) 'Can debt-reduction restore economic growth in highly indebted countries?' *Revue Economique et Politique*, 4(July–August): 639–66.

Mosley, P. (1996) 'The failure of aid and adjustment policies in sub-Saharan Africa: Counter-examples and policy proposals', *Journal of African Economies*, 5(3): 406–43.

Mosley, P., Harrigan, J. and Toye, J. (1991) *Aid and power: The World Bank and policy-based lending*, London: Routledge.

Moss, T.J. and Chiang, H.S. (2003). 'The other costs of high debt in poor countries: Growth, policy dynamics, and institutions', Washington, DC, The World Bank, Issue Paper on Debt Sustainability No. 3.

Ndikumana, L. (2004) 'Additionality of debt relief and debt forgiveness, and implications for future volumes of official assistance', *International Review of Economics and Finance*, 13: 325–40.

Ndikumana, L. and Boyce, J.K. (2003) 'Public debts and private assets: Explaining capital flight from Sub-Saharan African countries', *World Development*, 31(1): 107–30.

Neumayer, E. (2002) 'Is good governance rewarded? A cross-national analysis of debt forgiveness', *World Development*, 30(6): 913–30.

O'Connell, S.A. and Soludo, C.C. (2001) 'Aid intensity in Africa', *World Development*, 29(9): 1527–52.

OED (2003) 'The heavily indebted poor countries (HIPC) debt initiative: An OED review', Washington, DC, Operations Evaluation Department No. 25160.

—— (2004) *The poverty reduction strategy initiative, an independent evaluation of the World Bank's support through 2003*, Washington, DC: The World Bank.

Pattillo, C., Poirson, H. and Ricci, L. (2002) 'External debt and growth', Washington, DC, IMF Working Paper No. 02/69.

—— (2004) 'What are the channels through which external debt affects growth?' Washington, DC, IMF Working Paper No. 04/15.

Powell, R. (2003) 'Debt relief, additionality, and aid allocation in low-income countries', Washington, DC, IMF Working Paper No. 03/175.

Presbitero, A.F. (2005) 'The debt-growth nexus: A dynamic panel data estimation', Ancona, Università Politecnica delle Marche, Cuaderno di Ricerca No. 243.

Ratha, D. (2005) 'Demand for World Bank lending', *Economic Systems*, 29: 408–21.

Sachs, J. (1989) 'The debt overhang of developing countries', in Calvo, G.A., Findlay, R., Kouri, P. and de Macedo, J.D. (eds) *Debt, stabilization and development: Essays in memory of Carlos Díaz-Alejandro*, Oxford and Cambridge, MA: Blackwell: 80–102.

—— (2002) 'Resolving the debt crisis of low-income countries', *Brookings Papers on Economic Activity* 1: 257–86.

—— (2005) *The end of poverty: How we can make it happen in our lifetime*, London: Penguin Books.

Sachs, J., Botchwey, K., Cuchra, M. and Sievers, S. (1999) *Implementing debt relief for the HIPCs*, Boston, MA: Center for International Development, Harvard University.

Schclarek, A. (2004) *Debt and economic growth in developing and industrial countries*, Lund: Department of Economics, Lund University.

Serieux, J. and Samy, Y. (2001) 'The debt service burden and growth: Evidence from low-income countries', Helsinki, Paper prepared for the WIDER development conference on debt relief.

Stiglitz, J. (1998) 'More instruments and broader goals: Moving toward the Post-Washington consensus', Helsinki, WIDER, WIDER Annual Lecture No. 2.

—— (2002) *Globalization and its discontents*, London/New York: Norton.

Ul Haque, N., Nelson, M. and Mathieson, D.J. (1999) 'Rating Africa: The economic and political content of risk indicators', in Collier, P. and Pattillo, C. (eds) *Investment and risk in Africa*, Basingstoke/New York: MacMillan/St. Martin's Press: 33–70.

UNCTAD (2000) *The least developed countries 2000 report. Aid, private capital flows and external debt: The challenge of financing development in the LDCs*, Geneva.

—— (2004) *Economic development in Africa: Debt sustainability: Oasis or mirage?* Geneva.

Vaubel, R. (1996) 'Bureaucracy at the IMF and the World Bank: A comparison of the evidence', *The World Economy*, 19(2): 195–210.

Weeks, J. (2000) 'Latin America and the "high performing Asian economies": Growth and debt', *Journal of International Development*, 12(5): 625–54.

White, H. (1996) 'Evaluating programme aid, introduction and synthesis', *IDS Bulletin*, 27(4): 1–13.

White, H.N. and Dijkstra, A.G. (2003) *Programme aid and development: Beyond conditionality*, London: Routledge.

World Bank (1998) *Assessing aid: What works, what doesn't, and why*, Oxford/New York/Toronto: Oxford University Press for the World Bank.

—— (2002) *World development indicators*, CD-ROM, Washington: The World Bank.

World Bank and IMF (2006) *Applying the debt sustainability framework for low-income countries post debt relief.* Washington, DC.

Index

Figures are indicated by **bold** page numbers and tables by *italic* numbers.

Printed in the United States
by Baker & Taylor Publisher Services